Kenneth L. Dextrom
April 1974

fishing the MIDGE

by
Ed Koch

freshet
press
ROCKVILLE
CENTRE
NEW YORK

Front Endsheet: Big Spring, Newville, Pennsylvania
Back Endsheet: Upper reaches of Big Spring, near the head of the spring

IBSN 088395-017-0

Library of Congress catalog card number: 72-92785

Manufactured in the United States of America

Designed by Joan Stoliar

To JoAnn

*for her encouragement, understanding,
companionship, and love*

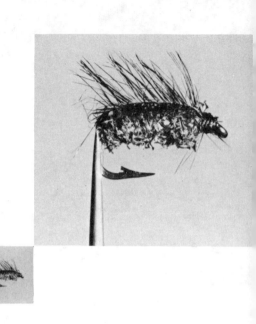

contents

foreword

BY JOE BROOKS

Ed Koch is one of the nationally known Carlisle fraternity of fly-fishers, students of stream life, and inventive tiers of flies to match the aquatic and terrestrial life of such famed old American streams as the Yellow Breeches, the Letort, and other limestone streams in Pennsylvania's Cumberland Valley. Out of their work have come many fly patterns and such outstanding books as Vince Marinaro's *Modern Dry-Fly Code* and Charlie Fox's *Rising Trout*. Now Ed Koch makes his distinctive addition to the scene with *Fishing the Midge*.

I have watched Ed tie these small flies and fish them with consummate skill, to bring up a two-pound brown to his tempting offering and then fight the fish to hand on a size-24 midge on a 7X tippet. From the tying, through the presentation and the battle, Ed knows every detail of every step of the way. In this book he describes the use of the midge, the ways trout take these very tiny insects, and the proper outfit to use when you fish them. He tells when to select the floating midge as your offering and when to go to the nymphal forms that swim just beneath the surface. Also included are a variety of excellent patterns and detailed descriptions of how to tie them. These fly patterns, mostly developed by Ed, a few by his friends, are new to the fishing scene. *Fishing the Midge* opens an unexplored field. It is the first book devoted entirely to midge flies. It's a book to read and reread and to make notes from. The pages to come are packed with information that will stand the serious angler in good stead when he reaches the river and finds the canny old browns and fresh, upstart rainbows feeding on "something too small to see." The information and patterns contained in *Fishing the Midge* will save the day for the fly-fisherman at such a time.

acknowledgments

It is difficult to recall all the angling friends who in one way or another contributed to the twenty years of fishing experiences that led to the completion of this work. To all of them I wish to give a heartfelt thanks, for without their companionship and advice this book would not have been written.

Special thanks are due to Bud Frasca and Mike Cohen of Freshet Press. Their initial encouragement and continued advice and assistance during the past two years have helped bring a dream to a reality.

I am especially indebted to Norm Shires, long-time friend and angling companion, for his outstanding photography, without which the over-all objectives of this book could not have been achieved. Our wives, JoAnn and Ruth, also deserve thanks for their patience and understanding during the long hours they have spent as angling widows.

I am grateful to Ed Shenk for the countless hours of his companionship, on the stream and off. I have been fortunate indeed to have had the privilege of fishing with and learning from Ed, who is surely one of the finest fly-fishermen this country has ever produced.

I would also like to take this opportunity of thanking my parents for introducing me to the joys of trouting and for instilling in me a deep-seated love and respect for the outdoors.

Finally, I would like to mention some of my thoughts and feelings as I reflect on my many memories of the late Joe Brooks. On the evening of August 20, 1972, I received a phone call informing me that Joe had succumbed to a heart attack earlier that day while fishing in Montana. Less than a week before I had spoken with him on the phone, and he had told me that his Introduction to this book was on its way to the publisher. He thought I'd done a good job and believed that the book filled a need and would be of interest to many anglers. That was the greatest compliment I have received in twenty-five years of tying, teaching, and writing.

By midnight I was able to inform my publisher of the tragic loss and ask him if it would be possible to insert a few more paragraphs, so that I might say something more of Joe than the acknowledgment I had previously written. His gracious reply was, "I'll hold it for your copy."

My closest association with Joe was through the Brotherhood of the Junglecock, an organization dedicated to teaching boys trout fishing and the preservation of this great heritage for future generations. Joe was the last living member of the original founding group. This is the Brotherhood's twenty-fifth anniversary year, and it is my privilege to be the current president. Joe had seen thousands of boys go through the three-day weekend, and it would be difficult to describe the pleasure he took in watching those youngsters learning fly-tying, fly-casting, and other angling skills. Joe would go out of his way, any time, any place, to assist a young angler on the path he so dearly loved.

My memory flashes back to years before I began to fish, when Joe was writing a five-dollar-a-week column for a local Baltimore paper. I remember his telling me about those early days when he was getting his start, and about the trip he made to Canada when he met Mary, who later became his wife and angling companion. His subsequent rise to fame earned him the title of the finest all-around fly-fisherman in the world. If ever anyone in the angling fraternity reached the top, Joe had. If ever anyone deserved it, Joe did. His character and devotion to the preservation of the sport were an inspiration to many, and will continue to inspire future generations. He will live in angling history as one of the great men who have gone before.

introduction

Trout fishing has been central to fishing with the artificial fly ever since, and no doubt even before, that day in the fifteenth century when Dame Juliana Berners first set down her list of "twelve flies with which you must angle for the trout." Over the years in which fly fishing evolved from primitive beginnings to its present high level of sophistication, the various phases of this wonderful art and sport have been the subject of much experiment and innovation. In particular, the insects that trout feed on have been widely studied, and many excellent fly patterns have been developed. Some aspects of matching the natural flies with artificials have been investigated as completely as it seems possible they can be, but in other areas much remains to be done. Midge fishing, for example, has been little written about. In the past twenty years, more and more fishermen have come to realize the fascination and unique effectiveness of fishing ultrasmall flies, yet this newest branch of the angler's art is still in its formative stages.

My stream notes and miscellaneous jottings were in a rather disorderly state when I started work on the manuscript that was to become this book. I had misgivings about putting my thoughts into print at a time when I had so much still to learn. But, I reasoned, to date no books specifically about midge fishing have appeared, and a start has to be made somewhere. So at the least, this work is a beginning. I hope it will inspire others who are involved in developing midge flies to make their findings known. I'm sure that, in years to come, much more will be written about midge fishing by others more qualified than I. These pages give a personal view of a large, rather new, and quite complicated chapter in the history of fly fishing. The material herein is drawn from notes and articles written over a decade. The task of organizing and amplifying this material turned out to be far more than I'd bargained for. The plan I finally settled on was to recount my own experiences of frustration, investigation, tying, and testing.

The title *Fishing the Midge* needs some explanation. I have used the word *midge* as fly fisherman use it. When a fisherman speaks of a midge, he usually means an artificial imitation of any small aquatic or terrestrial insect that a trout would find acceptable as food. Is the term correct? Is it misleading? It isn't really correct, but I doubt that fisherman will find it misleading. When entomologists speak of midges, they are referring to members of a family in the *Diptera* order of small two-winged flies. Mosquitoes and gnats also belong to families in the *Diptera* classification, and like true midges, they are aquatic in their immature forms. But whatever the correct usage of the word *midge* from the standpoint of the scientist, to fishermen the word has come to mean any very small artificial fly. Small mayflies, for instance, are extremely important to trout as food and to fishermen as models for certain small flies, but they are not midges in any technical sense. Nevertheless, fishermen often refer to small mayfly imitations as midges. In the course of my background work for this book, I read or referred to many American and English books on fly fishing, and whenever I came across the word *midge*, it was used to denote small fly imitations used to deceive trout. It mattered not whether the reference was to mayflies, caddis flies, *Diptera*, or terrestrials.

The small insects that midge flies imitate are sometimes referred to as *minutae*, a shortening of the Latin phrase *res minutae*, meaning things of slight importance. *That* term is certainly misleading, since the *minutae* are extremely important—to trout and trout fishermen.

As a fly fisherman, I've experienced a good deal of frustration over the years. You've probably seen your share of it too. I'm talking about those times when we know that trout are there in the water, but our finest conventional imitations, however well presented, just don't interest them. We all find ourselves in this daunting situation from time to time, and I suppose we all sometimes wonder whether we've lost our touch. The memory of such defeats can stay with you for years. We vainly dream that we'll be equal to this baffling predicament the next time it occurs. I don't necessarily mean that we want to catch and kill a difficult fish, but rather that we hope to deceive him with our imitation, to then release him, all the wiser, to play the game again. The real satisfaction of trout fishing eventually comes to that.

Writing this book brought to mind many happy memories of Pennsylvania's trout waters. I relived many days spent on Spring Creek, Elk Creek, Penns Creek, Fishing creek, Young Womans Creek, Kettle Creek, Slate Run, Pine Creek, Yellow Breeches Creek, Big Spring, Falling Springs, the LeTort, and dozens of others, including many small streams and beaver ponds that few anglers besides local people have ever fished.

Some recollections, though, were not altogether pleasant. Often I went home catchless and pondering after fishing a stream that I knew held many good trout. Such times set me to seining nymphs and catching duns and spinners in flight in an attempt to find reasons for my failures.

More recent memories are more gratifying, for my efforts finally began to bear fish. The answers were always found in the unnoticed. When fishing the Green Drake on Penns Creek or the March Brown on the Yellow Breeches or the Sulfur on the LeTort, I concentrated exclusively on the hatch that was most conspicuous, hardly noticing anything else that happened on the stream before, during, or after the hatch I was there to fish. But efforts at matching the conspicuous hatch would often come to little or nothing. Duns would be present and trout would be rising, but my imitations sometimes failed to entice a single fish. My flies weren't perfect, but I was satisfied that they were good, and one trout in ten, at least, should have been gullible enough to agree with.me. Yet now and then I caught nothing when conditions seemed ideal. Gradually I began to suspect that the fault wasn't with my flies or the way I presented them. It was just possible that these difficult trout were feeding on something other than the big flies that were so evident. I began to study the water more carefully, and my suspicions were often confirmed. A favorite hatch, let's say Cahills, was on the water, but so was something else—a hatch of very small flies that went unnoticed by ninety-nine per cent of the fishermen. These small flies were often more abundant than the more noticeable hatches, and at times the trout preferred the midges to the big, succulent flies. I can only suppose that trout sometimes find one sort of insect more appetizing than another. The feeding selectivity of trout is one of the most puzzling aspects of their behavior.

I am not an entomologist, not even in an amateur way, so very often I didn't know the names of the insects I was observing. My object was merely to tie convincing imitations, and to do this one need only copy the insect's size, shape, and color. My flies are meant to suggest the naturals, not to imitate then closely. I made the nymph bodies rough, without tails, legs, or wing cases. I kept the dry flies simple. In most instances they consist merely of tails, body, and hackle, though I found that a certain few flies need wings to be fully convincing.

With two exceptions (the cress bugs and the fresh-water shrimp) the naturals discussed herein are distributed generally over the northeastern United States. Very similar flies are found on trout waters nearly everywhere. The midge imitations discussed in the following chapters have worked very well over the years, not only for me but also for my friends and customers. I hope you'll find pleasure in tying and fishing them.

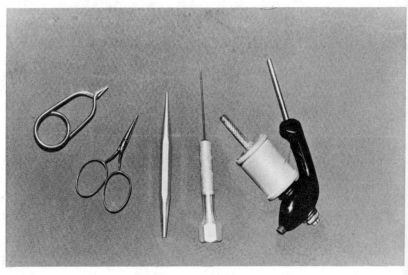

Hackle c, Scissors   Half-hitch   Bodkin or   Bobbin
Pliers   Tool   Dubbing
                                    Needle

tools and techniques

The fly-tying techniques and tools discussed in this chapter are basic. I offer no innovations, and many readers will be familiar with the methods I recommend, though some of the details may come as a surprise to inexperienced tiers. It's important that beginning tiers pay close attention to all the steps outlined. Proceeding slowly and thoughtfully at first will pay dividends later, when the fundamentals have become second nature.

Tools

Certain basic tools are necessary no matter what sort of flies you may want to tie. My years of experience as a fly tier (first as a hobbiest and later as a professional tier and as a teacher at tying clinics) have convinced me that certain tools often thought of as optional are essential if beginners are to do well enough at the outset to be encouraged to go on. Too often the novice becomes discouraged very early on because, without adequate tools and clear instructions, he finds himself unable to master the basics of manipulating fur and feathers.

A good vise is the beginner's most important and most expensive purchase. It must be capable of holding the smallest hooks. Don't pinch pennies when buying a vise. A good one will last for many years. Experienced tiers frequently own two vises, one for tying standard-size flies and another, smaller vise for midges. If you can afford it, a second vise especially for midges is a good investment.

A bobbin is a great advantage to anyone just starting out. No doubt many experienced tiers will disagree, but my work with beginners has convinced me that a bobbin is very helpful in enabling the new tier to manipulate the thread correctly while keeping the other materials under control.

A half-hitch tool is also a great aid to the beginner. This little implement is about four or five inches long and tapered and countersunk at both ends. One end fits over the ends of hooks in sizes 14 to 6 or thereabouts; the other end fits hook sizes 14 to 28. A beginner using a half-hitch tool will find that half hitching (putting in half a knot after each tying operation) is a very simple matter. The half-hitch tool can also be used to whip finish the heads of flies.

A good pair of scissors is another essential item. They should be from three to four inches long, with narrow blades and fine points that will cut well at the very tips. Larger scissors are too cumbersome for use on ultrasmall flies. A good pair of cuticle scissors will sometimes do.

Hackle pliers are also necessary. It's especially important to have a really good pair of hackle pliers when tying small flies. Get the best you can find. The jaws should be narrow and should hold firmly without cutting the hackle.

You will also need a bottle of *head lacquer*, or *head cement*, as it's sometimes called. A little head lacquer applied to the whip-finished head of the fly will insure that the thread doesn't unravel. A properly tied fly will almost always remain secure without lacquer, but it's best to play safe.

Two other items—*a dubbing needle* and a pair of *very finely pointed tweezers*—are very useful though not essential. Some fly-tying shops carry a good pair of tying tweezers with a dubbing needle attached to the handle.

A durable set of tools can be purchased for $25.00 or slightly less. This may seem like quite a lot of money, but consider this: as soon as you've tied four dozen flies, you'll have saved the price of the equipment. Ask any fly fisherman who fishes regularly how many flies he uses in a season. Good quality flies now cost about $6.00 a dozen, so you can see that it doesn't take long to go through $75.00 to $100.00 worth of flies. Many fishermen spend more than that on flies in the course of a season. The cost of fly-tying tools and materials is insignificant by comparison.

Besides saving money, fly tyers enjoy several side benefits. There is a fine sense of satisfaction that comes with turning out successful imitations. Every fly fisherman should experience the pleasure of taking his handiwork to the stream and for the first time catching a trout on a fly that he's tied himself. There's nothing like it. And it's a great feeling to be able to sit down at the vise and concoct an imitation for a local fly that just can't be found in the commercial market. Money can't buy the pleasure of accomplishment in trouting; involvement and work can. So to those of you who are just starting to tie flies—stay with it; the rewards are many.

Techniques

Fortunately, fly tying is not as difficult as most nontiers suppose. To the uninitiated, the knack of putting together various pieces of fur, feathers, tinsel, and thread so as to fashion a convincing fly seems a tricky, complex procedure. But it's really quite easy if you tackle the job in a logical, step-by-step way. It would be futile for a beginner to try to tie a hair-wing Wulff or a complicated salmon fly. The sensible thing is to begin with a very simple pattern. Once you've mastered the fundamentals, there'll be no pattern recorded that you won't be able to tie.

The numbered steps and illustrations in the chapters to come will take the reader through a series of quite simple ties, ending with the tying of a fairly complicated winged dry-fly midge. First let's consider a few basic techniques.

Securing the Hook in the Vise

The first thing to consider is the proper way to secure the hook in the vise jaws. This may seem obvious enough, but I've noticed that most beginners don't know how to do it.

Figure 1 shows a hook correctly placed in the vise. Notice that the entire bend is clamped in the jaws of the vise. The top edge of the jaws is positioned just below the point where the hook begins its bend. The lower edge of the jaws cuts across the lower portion of the bend. The barb of the hook protrudes from the vise head. This position is the only one that doesn't damage the hook in any way. When a hook is so placed, the vise exerts equal pressure along the entire bend, and the hook can't move up and down as the tier pulls on the thread.

Figure 2 shows a hook badly placed in the vise. Notice that the barb is completely concealed and only the lower half of the bend is covered by the

vise jaws. Some tiers position their hooks in this manner to keep the thread from catching on the exposed hook point. Covering the barb and hook point would be a good idea if it didn't weaken the hook and make for an insecure hold. When a hook is held as in Figure 2, the jaws apply pressure at only one point on the metal—right in the middle of the bend. If the jaws are tightened a little too much, they will crimp the metal at that point and weaken the hook. The chances are good that when the fly hits a twig or a stone it will break right off where the pressure was applied. And hooks with a crimped bend will sometimes break while a fish is being played. The small hooks used for midges are especially vulnerable to damage from the vise. Another disadvantage of this way of securing the hook is that the tension of the tying thread will cause the hook to move up and down as you tie. Many tiers have asked me why their hooks move around in the vise as they tie. They often want to know where they can get a vise that will hold the hook securely. When I ask how they put the hook in the vise, they almost always tell me that they use the method shown in Figure 2. When they switch to the method shown in Figure 1, the vise works fine. So it's far better for the beginner to learn to manipulate the thread around the exposed hook point.

This next operation is also very important. If the thread isn't properly secured, the fly will very likely come apart after little .use. On most of the flies one ties, the thread can be started at the rear of the hook shank. There are a few exceptions to this rule, but it really makes little difference where the thread is attached *if* it's properly secured. Practice the following four steps until they become second nature. (Please note that the instructions apply to right-handed tiers.)

Hold end of thread in left hand with bobbin in right hand.

1

Place end of thread below shank, hold bobbin above hook shank, and press thread lightly against hook shank.

Holding thread in position with left hand, wrap four to six turns of thread forward on hook shank.

Next wrap four to six turns of thread *backward* over wraps just completed. The overwrap will secure the thread to the shank.

2

Half hitch to complete securing. Clip off excess thread.

3

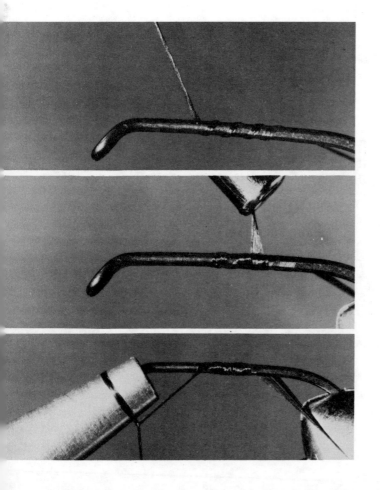

Using the Half-Hitch Tool

I call the half-hitch tool the fly tier's third hand. Half hitching and whip finishing can be done without the tool, but the beginner will find that it's a great help. You have the thread secured; now let's continue with the half hitch, which eliminates the possibility that the thread will come loose.

When the forward and backward wraps of the thread are complete, pick up the half-hitch tool in the right hand and hold the bobbin in the left hand.

Place half-hitch tool on top of thread.

Using the left hand, wrap one turn of thread around tapered end of half-hitch tool.

1

Slide half-hitch tool over eye of hook.

Pull thread off half-hitch tool onto hook shank and tighten. Half-hitch knot is complete.

2

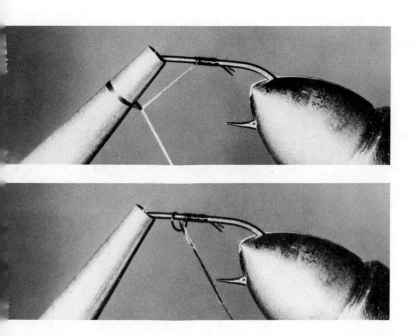

Tying on Tails

Attaching the tail is the next step in the construction of most flies.

Select a large hackle. Pull or cut fibers from hackle.

Measure fibers along hook shank to determine proper length. On a dry fly the tail should be a little longer than the hook shank. On a wet fly the tail should be a little shorter than the hook shank.

1

Hold the fibers in the right hand and position them on top of the hook shank at desired length.

Grasp fibers and hook shank with left hand and hold fibers in position on top of shank.

2

Holding bobbin in right hand, take two loose turns of thread around shank and tail fibers and pull tight.

3

Wrap a half dozen more turns of thread forward around hook shank and fibers, then half hitch to secure.

Clip off excess tail fibers, and tail is complete.

4

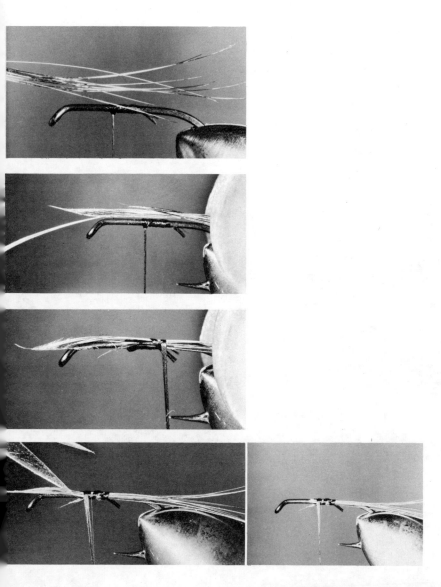

Dubbing the Fur Body

Clip small amount of fur onto table.

Pick up fur and spread it loosely over first three fingers of right hand.

1

Keeping fur on fingers, pick up bobbin in left hand and hold thread taut. Place fingers with fur against thread. Press thumb and forefinger together and spin fur on thread in a clockwise direction, applying pressure as you twist fur on thread. Dubbing is spun on thread and ready to wrap to form body.

2

Wrap dubbed thread in even turns two thirds of the way forward up hook shank, and half hitch to secure.

3

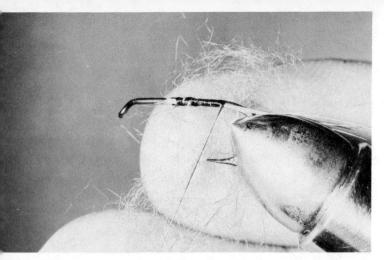

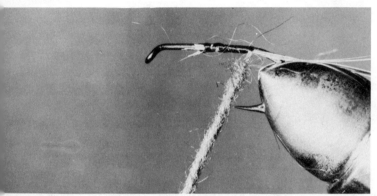

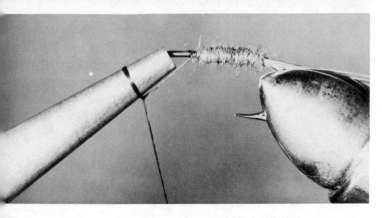

Tying Hackle-Tip Wings

Select two hackles from neck.

Measure tips of hackle along hook shank to determine correct length. Wings on dry flies should be a little longer than the hook shank; those on wet flies should be a bit shorter.

1

Strip off fibers, allowing two inches of stem to work with.

Holding stems in left hand, place hackles on top of hook shank with hackle tips pointing over eye of hook.

2

Wrap six or eight turns of thread over hackle stems, half hitch to secure,

3

and clip off excess stem.

4

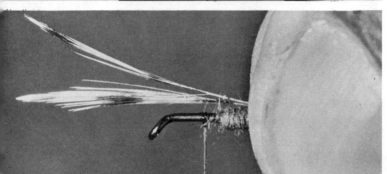

Grasp hackle tips in left hand and pull upright on hook shank. **5**

Wrap six or eight turns of thread in front of wings to keep them standing erect. **6**

Separate wings with bodkin. **7**

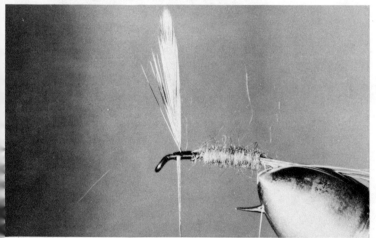

With left hand, hold wing furthest away from you and wrap three turns of thread behind wing nearest you and in front of wing held by left hand.

8

Hold wing nearest you with left hand or with hackle pliers held in left hand or with hackle in front of wing nearest you and behind the other wing.

9

You have now formed an X of thread around the wings. Wrap two or three turns of thread in front of wings and half hitch.

10

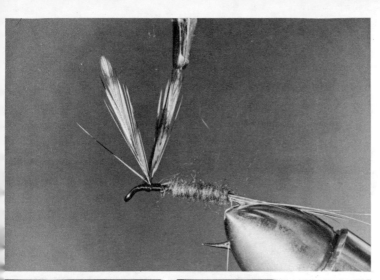

Tying on Hackle

Select proper-sized hackle—use a hackle gauge if you can't trust your eye—and strip away soft fibers on bottom third of hackle, exposing stem.

1

Tie in hackle by butt (stem), directly behind wings, if any, using six or seven close turns of thread, and clip off excess hackle butt.

2

Hold tip of hackle in hackle pliers and wrap two turns of hackle behind wings.

3

Now wrap two turns of hackle in front of wings. Tie off with several turns of thread and half hitch.

4

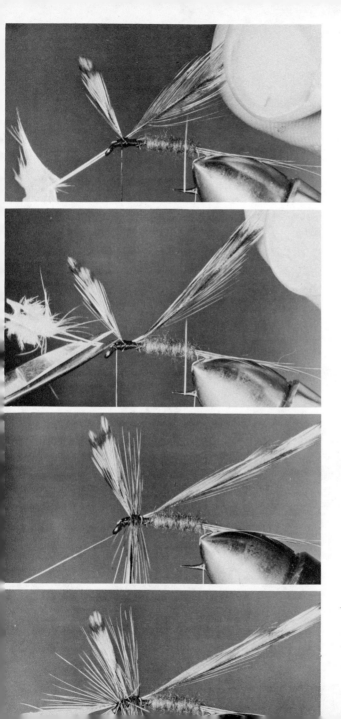

Clip off excess hackle tip. **5**

Wrap head, using as many turns as are needed to build a head of the correct size, and whip finish. **6**

Apply head lacquer with bodkin, **7**

and fly is complete.

Whip Finishing with Half-Hitch Tool

After fly is completed and head formed with thread, secure thread with half hitch.

Next, wrap three turns of thread on half-hitch tool. Pull thread from tool onto head of fly. On small flies three turns are enough if head lacquer is used. On larger flies you should put on three turns, pull off, and then put on three more turns before applying head cement.

To some readers the preceding instructions may seem awfully complex, while to others they may be old hat. If you're among the former, don't expect to be able to do everything right the first time; you won't be able to, and that's normal. Practice each step several times until you can comfortably manage the maneuvering of thread, fur hackle, and tools. Clip off the material each time you practice a step, then repeat that step. If you practice each step a half dozen times, you'll get the hang of it.

I suggest that you give this book a casual reading—I hope you enjoy it—just to get a general idea of what it's all about. Then go back and work on it chapter by chapter, tying the flies as you go. I think you'll find that this approach works best with most explanations of fly tying.

the
herl midge

Years ago the left and right branches of Young
Womans Creek were among the few waters in Pennsylvania where fly-fishing-only was the rule. These
two streams in the northcentral part of the state
were beguilingly picturesque, and the evening fishing was usually excellent. I spent many delightful
hours on this water.

It was on the right branch that I tested my first
midges. This branch had a fantastic evening hatch
of Green Drakes that started near the end of May
and continued till about the middle of June. My
wife and I reserved every weekend during this time
for a family campout on the stream. We looked
forward particularly to the spinner fall of Coffin
Flies at dusk. The evening fishing then was wonderful, but during the morning and afternoon it was
terrible. During the evening hatch and spinner fall
trout rose in extraordinary numbers, and long
stretches of the water boiled with rises. It was
almost incredible that the same water should appear so barren during the day. Most fishermen
would have given up long before the evening rise,

thinking there wasn't a trout in the stream. If JoAnn and I hadn't seen the evening's wild feeding, we would have thought so too. It was as though the trout had mysteriously vanished during the day and then just as mysteriously reappeared at night. This peculiar situation kept me baffled for the better part of two seasons.

One Saturday morning I fished upstream from camp, working the stream for about a quarter of a mile, and took only one trout. In the evening that same stretch of water would show more than a hundred rising fish. Feeling a bit dejected, I returned to camp. JoAnn hadn't started lunch, so I ambled back to the stream.

Near the camp a longish riffle flowed into a quiet pool. In the evening this stretch was one of the most productive places on the stream. The trout must certainly be there during the day, I thought, and there must be a way to catch them. I sat on the bank at the tail of the riffle, filled my pipe, and studied the water. Several minutes passed without incident, then at the head of the pool a trout rose. The rise was just noticeable—no more than a minute dimple in the surface. It wasn't till then that I noticed a swarm of tiny black flies hovering over the water at the end of the riffle. A minute later another rise came at the same place. During the next quarter hour the same small trout rose twenty-three times, and as I watched, seven more trout began feeding at the edge of the quiet water. They were taking the little black flies as they touched the surface. "Well, I'll be damned," I muttered to myself. I managed to grab a couple of flies out of the swarm. They were midges—minute two-winged water-bred flies that I later came to know well. I hurried back to tell JoAnn what I'd seen.

After lunch I got out my fly-tying kit and set to work. Rummaging through an assortment of fur, hackle capes, and miscellaneous feathers, I turned up a piece of black-dyed ostrich herl. This short-fibered herl seemed just the thing to imitate the blurred wing pattern of the midges. To match the size of the naturals I selected a size-22 hook with a turned-up eye. A few wisps of black hackle fiber would do to float the midge and simulate legs. Then I added the herl, wrapping it along the length of the hook shank. Not bad, I thought, knotting the fly to my leader, which I'd refined down to 6X. I tied four more just like the first, dropped them into my fly box, and hurried back to the pool.

All along the edge of the quiet water trout still cruised and rose. I chose a likely spot, worked out line, and made my presentation. The midge touched down about six inches to the side of a waiting trout. He darted over, snatched the fly, and headed back to his feeding station. The take came so fast that I was too startled to lift my rod tip; the trout hooked himself as the line came taut, and off he went, all over the head of the pool. He was small, but on a 6X tippet he had to be played a bit. In a few minutes I released a bewildered eight-inch brookie. The herl midge was a mess, its fibers wet and matted. I touched it up with a Kleenex and fluffed it back into shape. I was surprised to see that the sudden commotion hadn't put the other trout down. They were still busily feeding.

The next cast brought a trout up almost as promptly as the first had. He drifted over to the midge, inspected it, and confidently sipped it in. At the sting of the hook, he set off down the pool, shaking, splashing, and jumping. Soon I released a nine-inch brown.

I dried and fluffed the fly and cast again. Within a half hour the herl midge accounted for five trout. When I sat down to enjoy my new-found success, I couldn't help feeling a little foolish at not having paid closer attention to the water. Trout rising to midges often leave only a barely perceptible rise form, and you have to look carefully to spot them.

Now I was full of confidence. In three hours on the same stretch that in the morning had produced only one trout, I now brought fourteen to the net, all on the herl midge. Since then I've fished this midge regularly. Later experiments proved that versions of the same fly in gray, brown, white, and yellow ostrich herl are also very effective. There are about a thousand classified midges, and they come in a wide variety of colors. In these days of pesticides and stream pollution, many important mayfly hatches have either disappeared or been much reduced. The numerous small flies of the *Diptera* order seem more resistant to pollution than the vulnerable mayfly, and have thus come to have increased importance to fishermen bent on imitating the naturals. This pattern is so simple that beginners can turn out flies as good in every way as any of the experts could tie.

Tying the Herl Midge

BLACK HERL MIDGE
Hook—20 to 28
Thread—black nymph thread*
Tail—black hackle fibers
Body—black ostrich herl
Head—black nymph thread

BROWN HERL MIDGE
Hook—20 to 28
Thread—brown nymph thread
Tail—brown hackle fibers
Body—brown ostrich herl
Head—brown nymph thread

GRAY HERL MIDGE
Hook—20 to 28
Thread—gray nymph thread
Tail—blue-dun hackle fibers
Body—dun-gray ostrich herl
Head—gray nymph thread

YELLOW HERL MIDGE
Hook—20 to 28
Thread—yellow nymph thread
Tail—brown hackle fibers
Body—yellow ostrich herl
Head—yellow nymph thread

*The nymph thread called for in trying
all the patterns in this book is an un-
twisted, fine-stranded nylon thread made
by the Gudebrod Bros. Silk Co. Its diameter is equivalent to 8/0 tying silk, but
its strength is about equal to 6/0 silk. Its
property of flattening out when tied on
the hook makes it ideal for tying small
flies. It is available in black, white, gray,
brown, yellow, olive, and orange.

Insert hook in vise and attach tying thread directly above barb of hook.

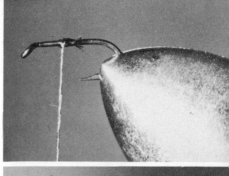

Select several hackle fibers and measure tail length along hook shank. Tail should be the same length as the shank.

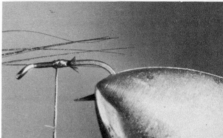

Tie on tail.

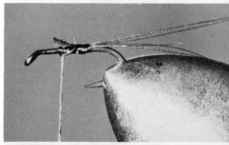

Select narrow strand of ostrich herl and tie on herl at bend of hook with three or four turns of thread. Wrap herl forward, each wrap as close to the preceding one as possible, to eye of hook. Tie of herl and clip away excess.

Build head with tying thread, whip finish, apply head lacquer, and fly is complete.

the wet
black ant

In the middle and late 1940s I spent much of my
fishing time on Spring Creek. The fly hatches then
were first-rate. Evening was the time for the best
hatches. During the day we fished a random assortment of dries, wets, nymphs, and streamers, merely
passing the time till the evening rise. We were
interested in catching and releasing as many fish as
we could, not in killing the biggest possible fish.
Our log still hangs in the kitchen closet of our
home back in the coal region. It records the dates
of our trips; the weather conditions; the flies we
used; and, in the last three columns, the number of
trout released by the three of us—my father, my
brother, and me. We all tied flies, and there was a
friendly rivalry among us as to who could tie the
most-successful patterns. We had some good days
and some bad ones, and we weren't much interested in finding out what made the difference.

One of our favorite flies was the old hard-back
ant, fished wet. Back then, we considered a size 14
small. Most of our patterns were tied on 12s or
10s. Over the years we tied the ant on smaller and
smaller hooks, and the smaller we made them, the

better they worked. Eventually we carried almost nothing but 18s, 20s, 22s, and 24s. We still kept a few 12s on hand, but I don't think we ever went back to the larger sizes. Using the small ants, we sometimes caught and released thirty to forty trout before sunset brought on the evening rise.

Almost always we cast to trout we could see. It was rarely necessary to fish the water. In the quiet water, trout lay in moss pockets and along the grass-lined banks, waiting for terrestrials to slip into the water. In the riffles and glides, other trout held in feeding stations where the fast water rushed over the wing walls and dams, bringing a steady supply of many types of insects. Working over these visible fish, we could usually see our flies as well as the trouts' reactions to them. In the slow water the rise, inspection, and rejection or acceptance were easily seen. In faster water, where the trout had only a few seconds to decide whether to take, we could often see a fish dart to one side or the other to gulp in the fly. Endless hours of this type of fishing eventually put a good deal of polish on our handling of short rods, small flies, and fine tippets.

I was then using a seven-and-a-half-foot glass rod and two-pound-test tippet material. Casting had to be accurate. In fast water the fly had to be placed close enough to the trout so that he could grab the artificial with a slight turn to one side. In quiet water the fly had to be placed so that it would drift to the trout without a suggestion of drag. We weren't catching the largest trout in the stream, but we were learning the finer points of casting, managing drift and drag, timing the strike, and— most important—observing the reactions of trout to the fly. For two lads of twelve and sixteen, all this was a wonderful challenge and a great experience. For many years, had anyone asked me to pick one fly to use all season long, I'd have promptly chosen the wet black ant. A supply of tiny wet ants always fills a compartment of my fly box.

Tying the Wet Ant

BLACK WET ANT
Hook—16 to 24
Thread—black nymph thread
Body—black nymph thread, lacquered black
Hackle—black wet-fly hackle

BROWN WET ANT
Hook—16 to 24
Thread—brown nymph thread
Body—brown nymph thread, lacquered brown
Hackle—brown wet-fly hackle

Insert hook in vise and attach thread to shank of hook directly above barb.

Wrap rear hump segment with thread and half hitch to secure.

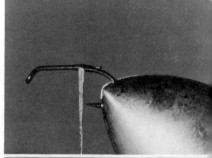

Apply drop of black lacquer with dubbing needle (on brown ant use clear head cement) and allow to dry.

Select wet-fly hackle, tie in hackle by tip, and clip off excess tip.

Wind two turns of hackle directly in front of rear segment, tie off, and clip off excess hackle stem.

Wrap front hump segment as in step 2.

Apply lacquer as in step 3. Allow to dry.

Whip finish head, apply head cement, and fly is complete.

grizzly hackle yellow

During the evening hatch on Spring Creek we usually fished the grizzly hackle yellow. We tied this fly with a yellow wool body and grizzly tail and hackle. We didn't bother with wings. As high-school lads we weren't concerned with turning out quality flies; it was quantity that interested us then. Wings were just too hard to tie, and we lost too many flies to be painstaking about tying perfect wings on a fly that might disappear with the first good trout that rose. Size 14 was what almost everyone used back then, but we eventually found that a size 16 was more productive.

The thrill of catching a trout on a dry fly made me forget everything I had observed during the day. I lost all tact when I should have most remembered it. Thinking that trout become careless during a hatch, *I* became careless. I made sloppy casts and often allowed the fly to drag. As a result, I hooked fewer trout than I did during the day, and of course just the opposite should have happened. Several seasons passed before I realized that the evening risers were even more finicky than the fish I was able to fool during the day. When I settled down to accurate casting and disciplined myself to keep alert during the whole day's fishing, I began to take more trout, and to take them more easily.

Eventually we began to tie the grizzly hackle yellow in size 18s as well as 16s, but we never tried smaller sizes. The 16s and 18s were good trout producers, and we were satisfied with them. We called this fly "the Dangler" because we often used it to practice a technique that we'd seen the old-timers use during the evening hatch. With four or five feet of leader hanging from the rod tip, the angler would scout the edge of the stream, watching for trout lying near the grassy banks. When a trout was spotted, the fly would be dangled out over the water and allowed to blow in the wind, touching the surface only sporadically. The angler would raise and lower his rod tip, "dapping" the fly on the surface. We were intrigued with this method, though skeptical at first, and we decided to try it. We found that "dangling" worked fine. Trout would sometimes jump six inches out of the water to get at the fly, hooking themselves on the way down. I still use this method occasionally, when conditions seem right.

When I moved to Carlisle, Pennsylvania, I found that two of the area's best fishermen, Ed Shenk and Norm Lightner, were using a fly somewhat like the Dangler. Their version, tied originally for the Big Spring at Newville, was an exceptional trout taker. It was designed to imitate several very abundant species of gray *Diptera*. Ed called it the No Name. (I've since learned that there are at least two other dissimilar patterns called the No Name. No matter.) Ed's No Name was tied with a body of light-gray muskrat fur and two or three turns of grizzly hackle. No tail was used. Sizes 20, 22, and 24 worked best.

Norm used to spend countless evening hours fishing the Big Spring. The hatch of gray midges was very regular and unbelievably heavy, and Norm was on the water whenever the little grays were. Using the No Name, he would fish a stretch of a hundred yards or so and in a good evening would catch and release a dozen or more trout.

I'm sure that Ed Shenk will also attest to the trout-taking powers of the No Name. He still uses them on the Yellow Breeches and the LeTort when all else fails. For me, the little gray has brought hours of fishing pleasure at times that would probably have been fishless without its help.

Tying the Dangler and the No Name

DANGLER
Hook—16 to 24
Thread—yellow nymph thread
Tail—grizzly hackle fibers
Body—pale-yellow spun fur
Hackle—grizzly
Head—yellow nymph thread

NO NAME
Hook—20 to 24
Thread—gray nymph thread
Tail—none
Body—gray muskrat fur
Hackle—grizzly
Head—gray nymph thread

Insert hook in vise and attach thread to hook directly above barb.

Select three or four fibers of grizzly hackle for tail. Measure length of fibers along hook shank and tie in tail. Tail should be just a little longer than length of hook shank.

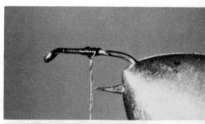

Tie on tail.

Dub small amount of spun fur on thread.

Wrap body three-quarters of the way up hook shank.

Select proper size hackle and tie in at hackle butt.

Clip off excess stem. Wrap two or three turns of hackle, tie off, and clip off excess tip.

Wrap head, whip finish, and apply head cement.

black and brown midges

For years the black ants and grizzly hackles in sizes 18 and 20 were the only small flies I fished. When I moved the Carlisle, in the heart of Pennsylvania's limestone water, the new techniques of midge and terrestrial fishing being developed there came as a revelation to me. Fishing the calm, tricky currents of the LeTort, Big Spring, Green Spring, and the Yellow Breeches was a fascinating new experience, and over the years it proved a great teacher.

The Yellow Breeches at Boiling Springs and the Big Spring at Newville both had large numbers of free-rising trout that seemed to prefer lies in the most problematical feeding stations. Fly presentation was often extremely chancy. These trout would lie for hours just under the surface, sipping naturals and blankly ignoring the hundreds of badly presented imitations that drifted over them. Occasionally—very occasionally—one of these wary fish would succumb to a size-24 wet ant.

One sweltering July afternoon I was fishing the deep water above the Allenberry dam. Trout were rising every twenty feet or so. They had taken up positions along the banks, under overhanging limbs, and even out in open water. It was as though someone were upstream chumming. I worked over these fish for nearly an hour, changing flies several times. The fish were easily spooked, and those I didn't put down stonily refused my offerings. I was ready to take up something saner than trout fishing.

Cradling my rod and lighting my pipe, I watched three trout feeding no more than three rod lengths from where I stood. They rose time after time. No trout can be that tough, I thought, peering through the smooth-flowing surface film for an answer to the problem. After several minutes a minute speck floated by. "*That* can't be what they're taking," I muttered, getting down as close as I could to the water. The little creature had darkish wings and a tiny black body that looked small enough to fit on the head of a straight pin. I got out my nylon specimen net and gathered a dozen or more of the little black specks. I picked them off the white cloth and put them in a collecting bottle. Back home, I looked them over with a 5X loop. The bodies were dark gray to black, the tails and wings dark gray to blue. Even a sparsely dressed size 24 might be oversized. I tied six imitations on 24s, the smallest hooks I had, and waited impatiently for the next day's fishing.

The next morning was clear, calm, and hot. The stream surface was covered with winged black specks, and the usual entourage of trout was break-fasting noisily. I waded into position below a rising fish. I had tied one of my new imitations to a 7X leader. The first cast was good. The midge drifted exactly to the trout. He took it, and I struck gently and deliberately. A nice trout shot out of the water, then rushed off, shaking to free himself. Several minutes later I released him, a plump, brilliantly colored brown.

The second trout, a smallish brookie, took the fly as quickly as the first. My presentation was off on the next cast, but the drift after that was good, and a third trout rose and was hooked. I went on to fish about a hundred yards of the quiet water and caught and released seventeen trout, the largest a sixteen-inch holdover. The black midge had earned a permanent place in my fly box.

I began using the brown midge after an experience much like the one that suggested the black. The little brown flies came out of a riffle just as it broke into a large quiet pool. The trout were as rigidly selective as they'd been when feeding on the tiny blacks. After drawing a blank, I got out my collecting net and gathered some specimens.

These flies varied in color from buff brown to light ginger. They didn't ride for nearly as long on the stream as the black ones had but hovered over the surface for an unusually long time before flying off to the trees and bushes along the bank. The trout were slashing at them, often coming clear out of the water. They turned out to be a legitimate size 20, though I've since seen similar flies as small as a size 26. I worked up two imitations. One is a brown variant, though without wings. The other is a bivisible. The variant tie has worked best for me.

Tying the Black and Brown Midges

BLACK MIDGE
Hook—20 to 26
Thread—black nymph thread
Tail—dark blue dun or black
Body—black nymph thread
Hackle—dark blue dun or black
Head—black nymph thread

BROWN MIDGE
Hook—20 to 26
Thread—brown nymph thread
Tail—brown or ginger
Body—brown nymph thread
Hackle—brown or ginger
Head—brown nymph thread

Insert hook in vise and attach tying thread directly above barb.

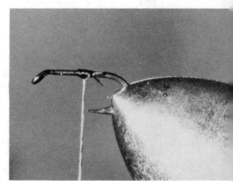

Select several hackle fibers for tail. Measure fibers along hook shank.

Tail should be a little longer than hook shank. Tie in tail and clip off excess.

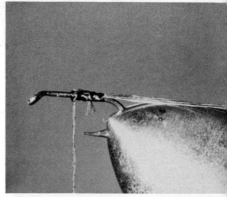

Wrap a smooth, even body of tying thread three-quarters of the way up the hook shank.

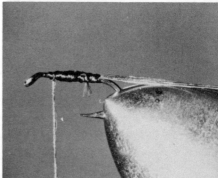

Select the proper size hackle. Strip off the soft fibers at the butt of the hackle, taking off the fibers to a point about one third of the way up the hackle stem. Tie in hackle by butt and clip off excess stem.

Wrap two or three turns of hackle, tie off, half hitch, and clip excess hackle tip.

Wrap a small head of tying thread, whip finish, and apply head cement.

a pair of
mavericks

During my early years in Carlisle I spent many evenings and weekends on the Big Spring and Green Spring near Newville. I'm sure that many readers are familiar with Big Spring. It was here that Don Martin took a brown trout of fifteen and a half pounds on a nymph. A brown of seventeen and a half pounds was caught there on a worm. Until the mid-1950s Big Spring was famous for its brook and brown trout population. In the late 1950s a commercial hatchery was established near its source, and since then there has been a marked decline in this once-famous water. Years ago it was nothing to fish pools containing fifty or more brook trout. Unfortunately, those days are nothing more than memories to the faithful Big Spring fishermen.

Green Spring, just a few miles away from Big Spring, is still largely unknown, even to many anglers living quite near Newville. A small stream, perhaps fifteen to thirty-five feet wide, it meanders through fields and meadows, winding its way to the Conodogoinet some two miles downstream. Today, given a choice, I'd spend my time on Green Spring rather than Big Spring.

Both streams are rich in aquatic life, and at one time they probably supported as many trout per acre as any water in the East. At certain times there were hatches of a size and variety to satisfy the most demanding dry-fly fisherman. There were also times when fishing was superb for anglers who could imitate the cress bugs and fresh-water shrimp that abound in rich limestone waters.

I began collecting cress bugs and shrimp from the LeTort, Big Spring, and Green Spring in the hope of working out successful imitations. Cress bugs range in size from about the diameter of a pencil to about that of a dime. They're grayish brown, flat, and roughly oblong. The shrimp are elongated, tapering down from the head to the tail, with small legs visible along the length of the underbody and a distinct fanlike spread at the tail. In color they vary from light to dark tan, and some have an olive cast. The smallest are almost too small too see; the largest reach a length of about five-eighths of an inch. They vary in diameter from about the thickness of thin pencil lead to about that of cooked spaghetti. The samples I collected lay for weeks on my tying bench as I ran up all kinds of eccentric concoctions in my attempts to imitate them.

Several patterns appeared to be just right, but hours of casting demonstrated conclusively that they weren't.

At about this time I began experimenting with bodies made of foam rubber. This material—the type that's used on coat hangers—is about an eighth of an inch thick and comes in various lengths, widths, and colors. I chose a gray piece for my cress-bug imitation. I found I could wrap narrow strips of foam rubber around the hook shank just as though it were wool, forming a contoured body. In fact, it could be tapered and stretched more easily than wool. I tied six cress-bug imitations in sizes 14 and 16, all with black herl collars and lines down the back. The herl was meant to imitate the bug's blackish head and the black vein that runs down its back.

The next Saturday morning found me in one of the upper meadows on Green Spring. The stretch I chose was a particular favorite of mine. It held a good number of trout and presented few problems in approach and casting. The stream there is fairly wide and about knee deep. It has a thick growth of cress and elodia. These water plants provide good cover for trout, and they're loaded with cress bugs and shrimp. Of all the places I'd sampled for specimens, this stretch seemed to harbor the largest populations of cress bugs.

At 8:00 a.m. I stood on the bank, sipping a cup of Thermos-bottle coffee and enjoying my pipe. Looking over the water, I decided to fish the right-hand bank, moving upstream, so as to have the sun at my back. In the first fifty yards of the water I meant to fish, a number of trout were feeding in the open channels that ran through the cress. If undisturbed, they would lie a few inches from the edge of the cress and feed for hours on the bugs darting in and out. Occasionally a trout would swim into the cress, shake his head, and drop back to gather the cress bugs he'd dislodged.

I approached a trout that was feeding just above me. I false cast once or twice and shot the line. The size-16 cress bug came down a yard to the left of the trout. He ignored it. I made a cautious pickup and cast again. I was sure the two-pound-test tippet was fine enough. This time the bug lit on the water a couple of feet ahead of the trout. The line of drift looked perfect. I couldn't see the fly, but the leader at the point where it sank would give me an indication of where it was. Just as the bug must have been drifting close, the trout moved to one side and opened his mouth. I lifted the rod tip sharply and felt the hook take hold. The trout whipped around and bolted past me, heading downstream toward a deep chute in the cress where he could tangle the leader. I arched the rod against him and pulled him up just short of the cress. It took me quite a while to bring him to net and release him. The second time I'd cast it, the new cress bug had brought me a deep-bodied fifteen-inch brown.

It's important that you watch the trout in this

Falling Springs

Herl Midge

Winged Ant

Wet Black Ant

Dangler

No Name

Black Midge

Brown Midge

Cress Bug Natural

Cress Bug

Fresh-water Shrimp

Twine Shrimp

Midge Nymph

Brown Midge Nymph

Caddis Worm

Midge Caddis Nymph

The Yellow Britches

Dun & Black Spinner

White Midge Spinner

White Midge

Little Olive

Blue Winged Olive

Caenis

Caenis Dun

Caenis Spinner

sort of fishing. You can tell from his movements, to one side or the other, backward or forward, whether he's about to pick up a bug. Even if he doesn't move, his gill covers will open and close as he opens his mouth to draw in a morsel of food. Though you may not be able to see your fly, you can usually tell when it's near your quarry. If the fish moves at all—strike. He's probably after your fly, and even if he isn't, your striking motion will make the fly dart toward the surface. Nine times out of ten, the trout will react as though the cress bug were trying to get away from him. Usually he'll grab it before it can escape. Dead drifting is an effective method, but sometimes a slight darting or swimming motion imparted to the fly will produce spectacular results.

I was fairly sure that I'd found the imitation I'd been looking for, but I couldn't be sure till I'd given the new pattern a thorough trial. Upstream from the first fish's station another trout was feeding. A rainbow, I thought. Creeping a little closer, I studied the current to see where the bug should be placed so as to drift to the fish. My first cast was far to the side, and the bug went past unnoticed. On the next cast the bug plopped down almost on top of the fish, and the leader went right over his back. He flashed into the cress and disappeared. I was annoyed with myself. Try to keep as much of the leader as possible out of the trout's window when you have the sun at your back. The thinnest nylon must look like rope to him.

When casting up and across stream, make your cast so that the leader curves somewhat to the side—to the left if you're casting to the left, and to the right if you're casting to the right. This will allow the fly to drop in front of the trout while the leader stays clear of him. That way you'll get a natural-looking drift and won't spook your fish. You can get your leader to curve by tilting your rod off the perpendicular as you make your forward cast. Tilt it to the right if you want a right curve, to the left if you want a left curve. Most right-handed casters can easily throw a curve to the right but have a little difficulty with the left curve. With left-handed casters it's just the opposite.

Moving upstream, I spotted another fish. The first cast was flawed but luckily failed to spook the trout. The next cast looked good to me but didn't bring a take. The third was way off the mark. On the fourth, the left curve fell perfectly, and I saw the fish take the fly. I set the hook, and he raced upstream, peeling off line. He stopped in midstream, rubbing his nose in the gravel, trying to dislodge the hook. The pressure of the two-ounce rod tired him quickly, and I released my second trout in fifteen minutes. The remainder of the meadow stretch produced seven more trout.

At the upper end of the meadow I sat and reflected on the morning's fishing. Not many things in fishing give more satisfaction than the successful working out of a new imitation. Pleased that my new fly was a success, I walked back to my car, feeling very enthusiastic about cress bugs. To the best of my knowledge, cress bugs don't inhabit freestone waters.   In limestone streams where the naturals breed in quantity, few flies are as consistently good. My prototype was a size 16, but I tie them now in sizes 16 to 22.

Tying the Cress Bug

Hook—16 to 22
Thread—gray nymph thread
Collar and back vein—black-dyed ostrich or peacock herl
Body—gray foam rubber cut into ¼'' strips
Head—gray nymph thread

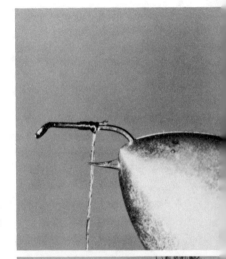

Insert hook in vise and attach tying thread directly above barb of hook.

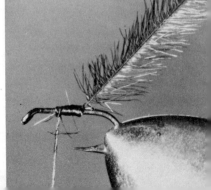

Tie in two pieces of peacock or ostrich herl at bend of hook.

Tie in strip of gray foam rubber at bend of hook, just in front of herl.

Wrap tapered body from bend to eye of hook. Tie off and clip off excess foam.

Pull herl forward over back of fly and tie off near eye of hook. Do not clip off excess herl. Instead, wrap a small segment of two turns of herl for head of bug. Tie off and clip off excess.

Wrap head of thread, whip finish, and apply head cement. Fly is complete.

I put off developing an imitation shrimp because the cress bug was new and accounting for a lot of trout. On some days, though, some of the more sophisticated Green Spring trout wouldn't respond to anything, and the cress bug began to lose some of its first luster. I began thinking about the shrimps I'd collected.

There were some shrimp patterns available from commercial tiers, but by limestone-stream standards they were far too big, and their colors didn't come close to matching our little fresh-water shrimp. I dressed down some of these patterns to smaller sizes, but they were no more successful than my own early concoctions.

I collected more specimens and studied them minutely, sketching and resketching their shapes and sizes on a drawing pad. I tried color matches with dozens of furs and hairs. Nothing looked right, and the trout were unconvinced. Then one day, rummaging around in my fifteen years' collection of fly-tying materials, I came across a small piece of brown hemp twine, the kind used in old-time hardware stores and feed mills for tying up packages. The color seemed a perfect match for the hue of our local shrimp.

Setting to work at my bench, I found that the hemp was too heavy to wrap into a satisfactory body on a size-16 hook, which was the largest size that would be suitable for a shrimp imitation. Another problem was that the stuff wouldn't dub properly. I solved both problems by untwisting the twine into three strands, then twisting each strand back into shape. The new pieces, each only a third the size of the original, could be wrapped into a tapered body on a hook of the right size.

To simulate the fan-shaped tail, I left a small section of the hemp extended beyond the bend of the hook and flared it with a dubbing needle. I tied the bodies in various shapes. Some I made even from back to front, others I made thin in back and fat in front, and a few I tied with a hump in the middle. They looked pretty good.

Frank Honisch and I had arranged to fish the LeTort on the coming weekend. Frank loved the challenge of the Letort. I've never seen anyone else who concentrates as hard as Frank on a good piece of fly water. Every other weekend for several years he made the two-hundred-mile round trip from Philadelphia.

As usual, Frank arrived early, which meant he must have left the city at around 5:00 a.m. After breakfast and some trout talk we headed for the LeTort.

Fishing upstream from Charlie Fox's house, Frank found quite a few surface feeders that fell prey to his delicately tied jassids and ants. It was a pleasure to watch him fish. His satisfaction was as obvious as his skill. Had Frank been a millionaire way back then, I'm certain he would have purchased the entire length of the LeTort, no matter what the cost, just to insure its preservation for years to come.

We were coming out of the woods below the S bend when I spotted a pair of trout in feeding stations along the far bank. They weren't surface feeding and wouldn't be enticed by any of Frank's perfect presentations. He moved on upstream. I stayed behind to study the two trout. Soon after Frank stopped casting to them, they settled down to feeding, darting back and forth between patches of cress. This seemed as good a time as any to test the twine shrimp. I cast to them for about fifteen minutes, persisting despite their indifference. I was ready to give up on them when on one toss the little shrimp sank in a pocket, drifted a short distance, and hung on a piece of cress a few feet ahead of one of the trout. I popped the fly loose. The rod lift and the current combined to roll the shrimp right past the trout. Again he ignored it. I was about to pick up the line when he turned downstream to the drifting shrimp, sucked it in, and headed back to his station. It happened so quickly and came as such a surprise that I didn't make a move. The trout hooked himself on the turn upstream. At the sting of the hook he dove with a swirl into the cress, where he slashed and tugged for several minutes. Steady rod pressure finally drew him into open water, where he immediately jumped twice. Frank turned at the sound of the splashes.

"What'd you get him on?" he called. Of all people Frank was the one I'd least like to have catch me out using a fly tied from binding twine.

"A secret weapon," I said. A few minutes later I removed the twine secret from the mouth of a fourteen-inch brown. Very promising, I thought, as the released brown darted into the cress. I waited a few minutes before trying the second brownie. It took a half dozen casts before he gulped the shrimp as it drifted by him.

That morning Frank caught and released thirteen trout, all taken on dries. My total using the twine shrimp was only seven, but I was tickled to death.

I fished the twine shrimp very hard for the next few seasons, and it proved to be one of the most consistent producers I'd used up till then. I still carry an assortment in sizes 16 to 22.

Considering the materials used in tying them, the cress bug and the shrimp are two of the oddest imitations I've come up with. They look a little disreputable, but they work.

Tying the Twine Shrimp

Hook—16 to 22
Thread—brown nymph thread
Tail—straw-colored twine or hemp rope
Body—straw-colored twine or hemp rope
Head—brown nymph thread

Insert hook in vise and attach thread directly above barb of hook.

90

Select piece of twine and tie in part way down bend of hook, allowing a small piece to extend beyond bend of hook. Wrap a body, starting halfway down bend of hook and wrapping forward toward eye. Begin to taper body on straight part of shank. Wrap forward to eye, tie off, and clip off excess.

Wrap head, whip finish, apply head cement, and clip tail to length. Fly is complete.

midge nymphs

Some of the first small flies I ever tied were standard patterns dressed down to midge sizes. These
miniatures weren't especially productive, but tying
them helped me get started on years of enjoyment.
Many of the standard patterns, such as Cahills,
Hendricksons, and March Browns, are meant to
represent species of mayflies that do not occur in
nature in midge sizes. To be maximally effective,
midge flies must be patterned after midge-sized
insects. The reasoning here is simple enough, and it
puzzles me now that this evident fact didn't occur
to me at the beginning of my experiments with
small flies.

Three of the first genuine midge patterns I
worked out were meant to be suggestive of certain

nymphal forms, rather than attempts at exact imitation. I called these first midge nymphs "Sim-fectives"—simple to tie and effective when fished. Read on and see whether you think these elementary miniatures would be worth tying up and trying out on your favorite stream. I think you'll be convinced.

A trout fly can hardly be simpler than these—no tails, no whisks, no feelers, no legs, no wing cases; nothing but a dubbed fur body. Sim-fectives are not really attractors, which are meant to intrigue or annoy trout by flashiness or novelty, but neither are they close imitations of specific nymphs. They're designed to suggest, by shape, size, and color, more than a half dozen different naturals. In their various colors they have a general resemblance to the nymphs of such small mayflies as the *Baetis, Caenis, Leptophlebia,* and *Callibaetis* genera, as well as to immature specimens of many other mayfly nymphs. After all, a Hendrickson nymph may be conventionally tied on a size 12 or 14 hook, but Hendrickson nymphs when only partly grown may be much smaller, and trout don't necessarily wait for nymphs to grow up before eating them.

The three basic colors for the great majority of all imitative trout flies are gray, brown, and cream. Consequently, I used three furs of these general colorations—muskrat, for dark-gray early season nymphs; weasel, for medium-brown mid-season nymphs; and fox, for late-season cream-colored nymphs.

These simple nymphs are remarkably effective, provided you're willing to do a little observing and practicing. The first step in using Sim-fectives is to check your local streams to determine the types of underwater insect life to be found there. This can be done with a small seine that you can buy or make yourself out of a piece of fine screen or nylon mesh. By holding the seine in a promising line of drift, you can collect a representative selection of nymphs by having someone dislodge rocks, silt, or underwater debris a few feet upstream from your net. The next step is to tie some nymphs that closely approximate in size and color the naturals that your collecting turns up.

I think you'll find that the most effective way to fish these midge nymphs is in the surface film or just below it. Let the fly drift on the surface without drag, just as though it were a dry fly. It won't quite float, of course. If properly tied, it will soak up enough water to sink slightly beneath the surface, possibly as deep as an inch or a little more. Grease your leader with Mucilin, or some other floatant, to within six inches of the nymph. This will keep the nymph drifting in the surface film or just under it. Keep your casts short or moderate. Beyond forty feet, a surface-drifted nymph is very hard to control, and detecting rises and making successful strikes becomes almost impossible. On the drift back, hold your rod tip high and keep your line as straight as possible, stripping in line at the same rate as the nymph drifts downstream. Only a few inches of slack should be allowed. That way you'll get a dead drift but still be in close contact with the fly. Watch the point where your line enters the water. I can't emphasize this strongly enough—keep that line point under close scrutiny at all times. When you see a tell-tale twitch, strike fast!

For every strike you detect, you can be sure that the nymph has been imperceptibly taken and ejected by at least a dozen trout. Here's where patience and close attention pay off. No one becomes an expert nymph fisherman overnight. With enough practice, you'll find yourself striking and hooking fish that gave so little sign of a take that the process seems uncanny. But that degree of sensitivity comes slowly. Nymph fishing is, after all, the most demanding of all forms of fly fishing. Once you've become an initiate, though, you'll find that no other method is as reliable or as deadly. A good nymph fisherman can take trout when others are convinced that *nothing* will bring a strike. Again: watch like a hawk for the slightest sign of a rise, and strike quickly. Unlike dry-fly fishing, nymphing calls for a sharp, instantaneous strike. Anything less than an immediate reaction will usually give the trout time to appraise the morsel and spit it out.

Writing about midge nymphs brings to mind an experience in which one of them, the weasel-fur nymph, turned what might have been a disappointing trip into a pleasant memory. My wife and I had driven to Manchester, Vermont, on a jaunt that combined fishing, antique hunting, and business with the Orvis Company. It was mid-July. After checking into a motel, we browsed through the Orvis store, then drove to the factory to chat with Dick Finlay and Wes Jordan. Dick and Wes were glad to see us but discouragingly negative about our prospects for good fishing. There had been a dry spell, and the river was low and clear. Vermont was having an unusually hot summer, and the fishing had fallen off. Wes and Dick thought that we should wait for the cool of the evening, but I was eager to get on the Battenkill. I asked JoAnn to drop me off at the bridge at Manchester Center, where I planned to fish for two hours while she went off to scout the antique shops.

I stood on the bridge and scanned the water. There wasn't a sign of activity. The river was so quiet it seemed almost stagnant.

A hundred yards or so downstream from the bridge is a long, quiet pool thickly fringed with mountain laurel. The laurel had grown up to over six feet and came together at the top, forming a canopy over the water. Inside this lush green tunnel the water was deeply shaded. It would be cooler there. I walked to the lower end of the tunnel and entered the river. The water felt cold through my waders.

Standing motionless, I peered into the leafy tunnel. After a moment I noticed a tell-tale ring widening as the current carried it downstream. Would it be a chub or a trout? Another ring appeared, then another. Soon I saw that five fish were steadily rising. I looked for whatever was causing the rises, but saw nothing. Strange, I thought. Very strange. Those are definitely rises up there. It could be that the fish are coming up to something too small and dark for me to see in the shade. Or to minute terrestrials. Or small nymphs. Could be any one of a lot of things. But what? The fish kept on feeding.

Playing a hunch, I tied a size-18 Shenk's Special to my leader. This little creation is no more than a body of dubbed weasel fur ribbed with extra-fine gold wire. I considered this tail-less, wingless, thoraxless little nymphet and decided that it ought to drift a bit under the surface. The rises didn't look like typical surface rises. I soaked the nymph briefly and waded to the left bank of the river. My plan was to use a sidearm cast to get the fly across toward the right bank and up under the overhanging foliage.

Close in toward the left bank and some twenty feet up ahead of me a tiny ring appeared on the surface. I flipped out two false casts and painted the line on the surface as delicately as I could. The nymph came down just above the drifting rise form. It scarcely had time to sink when a trout swirled under it. I lifted the rod tip reflexively and felt the tug of a good fish. There was a waterside tangle of brush on the far side of the stream, and that's where the trout headed. I put on as much pressure as I thought the 6X tippet would stand and managed to keep him in open water. When I had the fourteen-inch brown in my net I saw that the little nymph was firmly imbedded in the roof of his mouth, a sure sign of a good take.

In a few minutes the pool had settled down and a fish resumed feeding, this one in mid-stream and a few feet upstream from where the first had appeared. I tossed the fly—*plip*, it landed right in the ring—and another swirl came just under the surface. I was fast to an eleven-incher. After releasing him, I paused to light my pipe and think the situation over. The water was low and warm, the weather hot. No more than a half hour before, Wes had told me that days had passed since there'd been any activity worth mentioning. Yet these trout were taking as though they were starved. Certainly no one had been wading this pool recently. Again I searched the water for whatever the trout were taking. The surface film appeared empty of insect life. I wondered whether those two fish had been accidents. Maybe I'd already caught my quota for the day.

Three more rings appeared upstream, two near the right bank and one in mid-stream. *Plip*—the nymph hit the water beside the nearest ring. There was a swirl and a wake arrowed toward the fly. The third trout turned out to be a ten-inch brookie. I cast to the fourth trout, had another immediate take, and soon released a ten-inch brown. Number five was his twin. I had fished about ten yards of the river, and every cast had produced a trout. It was a curious situation, all right, and almost too good to be true. Totally engrossed, I worked upstream, unaware of time passing.

Suddenly the shady peacefulness of the laurel tunnel was broken by three sharp blasts of a car horn. It was JoAnn's signal that two hours had gone by. I walked to the bridge, feeling very fine. JoAnn asked how I'd done.

"Not bad," I said. "Not bad at all." I showed her four twelve-inch trout that I'd killed for the owners of the motel. Two hours of fishing had produced eleven trout.

Back at the factory I told Wes about my experience. He could hardly believe it, and if I hadn't produced those four trout as evidence, I'm sure that he'd have thought the heat had gotten to me.

"What were you using?" he asked

"This." I held up the sodden little nymph.

He examined the fly. "I'll be damned," he said. "It looks like a little wood worm."

I don't know what Wes had in mind when he referred to a wood worm, but I suspect that the trout in the Battenkill are familiar with them. Just before we left, Wes stuck the fly in his hat for a sample.

Tying the Midge Nymphs

 GRAY MIDGE NYMPH
Hook—16 to 28
Thread—gray nymph thread
Body—muskrat fur
Head—gray nymph thread

BROWN MIDGE NYMPH
Hook—16 to 28
Thread—brown nymph thread
Body—weasel fur
Head—brown nymph thread

CREAM MIDGE NYMPH
Hook—16 to 28
Thread—yellow or brown nymph thread
Body—cream fox fur (belly of red fox)
Head—brown or yellow nymph thread

Insert hook in vise and tie on thread at rear of hook shank, directly above barb.

Dub a small amount of fur, guard hairs and all, on thread.

Build an evenly tapered body forward to eye of hook and half hitch to secure.

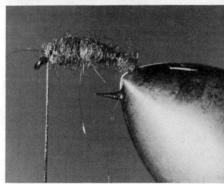

Build up head, whip finish, and apply head cement.

midge
caddis
nymphs

The evening hatch was about to start. A few flies were already coming off the water. Birds were flying excitedly about, and here and there a trout had begun to rise. I stood where a fast riffle tumbled over large boulders and poured into the head of a long, deep pool. The current was strongest on the far side of the pool. That was where the main feeding lane would be. The far bank was steep, almost impossible to walk along, and thickly grown up with brush. The trout would have good cover there in stations just a few feet from the main current. I kept motionless, watching, as several trout rose within thirty feet of me.

A trout was feeding at the edge of the current. He had taken up a position at a point where the main force of the water swept around a broken tree limb dragging in the stream. I could see exactly what he was doing. His rise wasn't the gulp or slurp of a trout taking a floating dun from the surface. Instead he rose into the surface film, opened his mouth wide, and stuck the tips of his jaws up just far enough to break the surface, causing the familiar break and ring that many fishermen mistake for a true surface rise. He was taking the emerging nymphs just beneath the surface. He had only to move a few inches this way or that to catch the helpless nymphs as they struggled to shuck their cases, activate their wings, and pop out on the surface as duns. When feeding on nymphs at this stage of their emergence, trout open their mouths wide and take in some water along with the emerger. They then expel the water through their gills, swallow the food, and settle back to their observation posts to wait for another tidbit. The fisherman who can distinguish this type of rise from the real surface rise can enjoy hours of fun, fishing the nymph in the surface film. It's semi-dry-fly fishing, a most productive method once mastered.

Feeling fairly sure of myself, I dropped my size-14 gray caddis nymph about two feet above the trout. It floated within six inches of him. He looked it over and dropped back into position. Drag, I thought. The next cast sent the fly drifting free of drag right down the feeding trough, over the trout's head, and downstream untouched. All right, I thought, must be the wrong size or the wrong color. Should I try the same size fly in a different color or the same color in a different size? Most fly fishermen I talk with tell me that in such situations they normally switch to a fly of the same size but a different color. That's where many otherwise competent anglers make a mistake. If you know your water and know which flies are likely to be hatching at different times in the season, it's only logical that you should stick with the color fly that best matches whichever insect you expect to be on the water. The best policy, of course, is to do a little collecting and see for yourself what items are on the trout's bill of fare, but sometimes we haven't the equipment or the time or the patience for such work. I peered into the water, hoping to see what was carried in the surface film. Nothing was evident. I was sure that the nymph of the fly about to hatch would be either a 14 or a 16. There wasn't a sign of any such creature. The trout rose twice more, and still I had no idea of what he was taking.

Often when a fisherman has his fly rejected several times he begins to act as though he'd been refused by the last trout he'll ever have a chance to cast over. He panics, changes flies, casts, changes flies again, casts again, and completely forgets such matters as accuracy, delicacy, and pattern size, which at such moments are critical. He usually puts the trout down. If he can calm those jangled nerves and take time to think, he'll often come up with a solution. Let's get on with my problem, and I'll show you what I mean.

I overcame my impatience and got out my nylon-mesh collecting net. This net is about eight inches long and looks something like a miniature windsock. It has a piece of spring steel sewn into the top to keep the mouth open. I held the net in the water for a minute or so and then checked its contents. Leaves, twigs, bits of grass, and a few tiny gray specks clung to the mesh. The specks were caddis nymphs, about a size 20. It was easy to see why the trout had ignored a larger fly.

I had been expecting a hatch of caddis flies of about a size 14, but my collecting foray had produced only size 20s. I watched the trout rise several more times and promised myself that I'd do a little more research after another try at that canny riser. Taking my cue from what had turned up in my net, I tied on a 6X tippet and attached a size-20 gray midge nymph. The cast and drift were good. Up came the trout, but this time, instead of turning away, he opened his mouth, flared his gills, and slipped back into position. I brought the line taut and had him hooked. After about five minutes of struggling against my two-ounce rod he came to net. A fat, bright-hued brown was my reward for twenty minutes of trying. Definitely a holdover from last year, I thought, as I slid him back into the water.

Putting aside my intention of doing some more collecting, I immediately tried the nymph on another trout. During the rest of the afternoon the nymph produced only spotty results. It worked fairly well, but it wasn't sure-fire. Before quitting

for the day, I went back to work with my specimen net and gathered a good number of little
caddis nymphs. Most were less than an eighth of an
inch long. They varied in color from black to gray
to dirty brown and olive. Many had a distinct tiny
black head. Some had legs, others were legless.
None had visible tails. I bottled the specimens and
stowed them away.

Later, at my tying table, I set about fashioning a
really convincing imitation. I decided that the
nymphs should have herl heads and slightly tapered
bodies. For hooks I chose Mustad 7948As in sizes
16 to 22. To approximate the different body
colors, I used a variety of furs—muskrat, rabbit,
bobcat, fox, and oppossum, as well as dyed furs in
blue-dun gray and olive. I tied six flies in each of
the four sizes.

Below the Allenberry dam on the Yellow
Breeches the water rushes and swirls in several
types of runs. Fast water churns the stones and
gravel and the debris from the breast of the dam.
Trout here have a continual supply of food washed
to them. Often they lie in slack water, now and
then darting into the current to grab something
that looks edible. This stretch gets fished harder
than any other in the area. Trout here are as
familiar with anglers' deceits as any trout can be.
They must see thousands of hopefully cast imitations every season. The early morning hours are the
best time to fish this water, though even then the
pool is sometimes crowded with fishermen.

I tested my midge caddis nymphs here one Sunday morning in late summer. Conditions were just right. There wasn't another fisherman in sight. The sun had just come up on the creek, giving me a good view of the trout. All I needed was an hour or so without anyone disturbing the pool. I made a careful approach into the tail of the pool. A dozen or more trout were lying in knee-deep water and feeding hungrily.

On my first good presentation a trout moved toward the nymph, a size-18 gray. I could see him clearly. He swam up to the nymph and took it as though he were being hand fed. I was too fascinated to react. He appeared to munch the nymph appraisingly before spitting it out. Intrigued, I stopped fishing to watch the trout. They would pick up something that was drifting by or that lay on the bottom, mouth it, to see whether it was good, I suppose, and then either spit it out or swallow it. This would be a very interesting session if the trout remained as easy to see as they were at first. I tossed my nymph to the trout that had already taken it once. He took it as casually as before. This time I was ready. Once hooked, he turned into the current and ran for deep, fast water. The strong current and the deep bow in my rod quickly tired him, and as I bent to release him I saw that the nymph was firmly hooked in the roof of his mouth. The second trout swam well to the side to pick up the nymph. Time to change colors, I thought, releasing him. I switched to a dirt-brown nymph tied with bobcat underfur. Within fifteen minutes it accounted for three more trout. I continued to change flies. The cream nymph didn't interest the trout at all, but the olive took five. By the time another fisherman arrived at the pool, the little caddis nymphs had duped eleven fish.

I wondered whether my new creations would work well in fast water, where all that can be seen of the fish is the occasional flash of a trout working in the riffles. Perhaps they'd be too small for the trout to see. Upstream a half mile or so is a section of broken water that often has a good hatch of caddis flies. Here the stream bed narrows, and the current roars through its thirty-foot width. I drove up to this stretch to give the nymphs a final test. I tied on a size 16, thinking that a smaller size would be swept along too fast for the trout to see. I stood near the head of the fast water and made my casts across and upstream, letting the fly drift naturally for fifteen or twenty feet. On the third or fourth cast the leader stopped near the beginning of the drift. I struck promptly, and a good-sized fish rushed downstream, peeling off forty feet of line before stopping to hold in the current. I backed off and waded downstream to get below him. It took me ten minutes of spirited tussling in the fast water to bring in a shining sixteen-inch rainbow. Several more good fish fell to the size 16 before I decided to change to one of the smaller sizes. The size-18 bobcat nymph produced five trout within a short stretch of fast water.

At the end of the run the fast water fans out into a shallow glide. Trout were holding here in the slack water near the opposite bank. I decided to try a size 20. Casting across the current and getting the nymph to drift naturally was a difficult business. the fly would drift only a few inches in the slow water before the mid-stream fast water bellied the line and sent the fly dragging wildly past the trout. Placement had to be exact, to take advantage of the short natural drifts. I made dozens of casts before I placed one just right. Out darted a trout. Not much of a strike is needed in such circumstances. The fast water will usually set the hook, and that's what happened here. Fifty yards of this water produced seven more trout, all on the size-20 caddis nymph. Another miniature pattern had proved its value. The four basic colors of gray, brown, cream, and olive are all excellent trout takers.

Tying the Caddis Midge Nymphs

GRAY CADDIS NYMPH
Hook—16 to 24
Thread—gray nymph thread
Body—muskrat fur
Head—peacock herls

BROWN CADDIS NYMPH
Hook—16 to 24
Thread—brown nymph thread
Body—bobcat fur
Head—peacock herl

CREAM CADDIS NYMPH
Hook—16 to 24
Thread—brown nymph thread
Body—cream fox fur
Head—peacock herl

OLIVE CADDIS NYMPH
Hook—16 to 24
Thread—black nymph thread
Body—olive spun fur
Head—peacock herl

Insert hook in vise and attach thread directly above barb of hook.

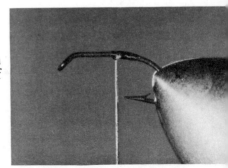

Dub small amount of fur on thread. Wrap evenly tapered body forward to eye of hook and half hitch to secure.

Tie in single strand of peacock herl.

Wrap two or three turns of peacock herl for head.

Tie off and half hitch to secure.

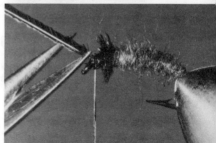

Wrap head with thread, whip finish, and apply head cement.

dun and black spinner

The three trout kept to a steady rise rhythm. I had been casting to them for almost an hour. I had changed flies at least a dozen times, switching from dries to terrestrials to midge nymphs, and hadn't provoked a single rise. It was late May on the "fly area" of the Yellow Breeches. The trout had looked over a size-20 black midge, a size-24 black ant, and a size-20 midge nymph, but each time they'd turned away at the last second. I was sure that the casts had been well placed and delicate and the floats just right, so it couldn't have been my presentation that was at fault. The trout hadn't been spooked; they went right on feeding. That in itself was a small triumph. If I'd been in the same predicament a few years before, the trout would have been put down early in the game. Exasperated,

I snipped the midge from the 7X tippet and for the fifth or sixth time stared at the water, straining to see what the trout were taking. I looked hard for several minutes, my eyes only inches from the surface. I couldn't see an insect of any kind. Was it possible that those trout weren't really feeding but only rising to keep in practice?

In desperation, I pulled Don DuBois's match-the-hatch net out of my vest pocket and held it in the current. The water had seemed empty of fly life, but I should have looked longer and harder. Clinging to the net was a tiny black spinner with extended wings. The wings and tails were dun gray, the body slender and black. I looked at the surface again, and knowing now what to look for, I immediately saw them—minute spinners, all perfectly spent, floating by in good numbers. Of the flies I'd been using, the little black ant had looked the most like the spinners, and it had seemed to interest the trout the most. Were these trout so sophisticated that they could tell the difference between a spent spinner of about a size 26 and a dubbed-fur ant of nearly the same size? It seemed farfetched that trout could be that selective. There was nothing in my fly box that looked like a good match. For want of something better, I tied on a size-28 gray midge. I gave up after twenty minutes of useless casting. Might as well go home and tie a few, I thought.

The only really small hooks I had at the time were gold-plated 28s and bronzed 24s. Would the bright gold be noticeable in so small a fly? To be safe, I decided on the 24s sparsely dressed. I used three hackle fibers of dark-blue dun for the tail, black nymph thread dubbed with fine black fur for the body, and a tiny dun hackle tied variant style. To simulate the spent wings, I trimmed the top and bottom of the hackle after it had been tied on the hook, leaving just a few fibers extending on the sides. The completed fly looked near enough like the original. I tied three more and hurried back to the stream.

The three trout were still at it, mopping up the little black spinners. I lengthened my leader to twelve feet by adding a 7X tippet, and waded into position. It seemed best to let the commotion of my wading quiet down a bit. I lit my pipe and waited. How many times in the past year had I gone through the same elaborate routine of observing, collecting, tying, and testing? At least fifty times, I was sure. Often the effort had been wasted, but the eight or ten successful patterns I'd developed made all the experimentation worth while. Investigating trout behavior and searching for new patterns gives me as much satisfaction as hooking, landing, and releasing a wise old brown. Each promising new midge was tested time after time on various waters, and only those that consistently fooled the smartest trout were made permanent residents of my fly box. The collection was small but select.

The trout nearest me was rising often now. As I watched he came up three times in quick succession. I dropped the fly a few feet ahead of his last ring. The float was to his left, but just as the fly came even with him he turned, moved up—and hesitated. Straining to see, I muttered, "Take it, take it," and as if on command, his jaws opened and a small dimple appeared where the fly had been. He was a husky foot-long brown and put up a mettlesome fight before I released him. Even the most selective trout will cooperate if you can come up with exactly what he wants.

As always when a new pattern has its first success, I wondered whether I'd solved a problem or merely been lucky. It wasn't luck. Four more ultra-cautious trout rose to the new fly that day. All through that summer, whenever I couldn't interest our hard-fished local trout, I'd look for the little dun and black spinners. Often I found them, and whenever they were on the water the new fly took fish. Needless to say, the little spinner has become one of my mainstays.

Incidentally, this book had almost been completed when Leigh Perkins and Tony Skilton of the Orvis Company came to Allenberry for a weekend of fishing. At dinner one night Tony asked me whether I'd like some size-26 hooks. Thinking he was putting me on, I said, "Sure, I'll take a thousand as soon as you get back." He wasn't kidding. It turned out that Orvis is now handling Mustad size-26 hooks. Bronzed, not gold! Sizes 20, 22, 24, and 28 are relatively easy to find, but 26s have been a rarity. These hooks should fill a conspicuous need of midge tiers and fishermen. Patterns calling for a sparsely dressed 24 can now be tied on 26s.

Tying the Dun and Black Spinner

Hook—24-26
Thread—black nymph thread
Tail—dark gray dun hackle fibers
Body—black spun fur
Wing—dark gray dun
Head—black nymph thread

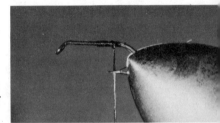

Insert hook in vise and attach thread directly above barb of hook.

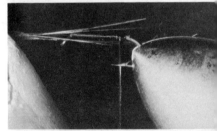

Select three dun hackle fibers for tail. Measure along hook shank.

Tail should be as long as hook shank. Tie on tail, half hitch, and clip excess.

Wrap dubbed fur body three-quarters of the way forward on hook shank, tie in, and half hitch.

Select proper size hackle, remove soft fibers from base and tie in butt of hackle.

Wrap three or four turns of hackle, tie off, and clip excess hackle.

Finish head, whip finish, and apply head cement.

Clip V in top and bottom of hackle.

Completed fly, top view.

the
white midge

In 1961 the Yellow Breeches Anglers' and Conservation Association was formed at Boiling Springs, Pennsylvania. One of its main objectives was to improve local fishing. The Association was one of the first groups to become involved in the Pennsylvania Fish Commission's "cooperative nursery" programs. A site for a nursery was obtained from Homer and Alma Thornton, long-time residents of Boiling Springs. The Association raises 30,000 trout a year and stocks them in seven miles of the Yellow Breeches.

A fly-fishing-only area was petitioned for and established just below the town. I doubt that anyone gave much thought to researching a site for the regulated water, but even if the Association members had deliberated for a year, they couldn't have come up with a better choice than the present mile of water. The upper end of the fly-only area starts where Boiling Springs Lake pours fifteen million gallons of water a day into the Yellow Breeches. The source is the underground springs that feed the ten-acre lake. The water is clear and pure and stays cold on the hottest summer days. The average year-round temperature is in the low 50s. Consequently, the fly-only water is the richest, most productive stretch in the thirty-seven miles of the stream.

During the past ten years, more than seventy per cent of my fishing has been done on the fly-only water. The river has been a gracious host. Trout abound. The quantity, quality, and variety of insect life surpasses that of any water I've fished in the eastern United States. Several seasons of fishing and observation on this wonderful river can only begin to reveal its bounties and natural potential. Considering our present ecological crisis, the value of this water is inestimable.

Some regulars on the Breeches are convinced that natural reproduction occurs in the stream, though not nearly enough for the water to support the heavy fishing pressure it receives. But the fact that a capacity for natural reproduction exists makes the Yellow Breeches exceptional among civilized trout waters. I hope one day to write at length about the river. I'd like to do all I can to contribute to its preservation for future generations.

What a classroom the Yellow Breeches has been! Few streams have such a diversified abundance of fly life. Here one has opportunities to fish such hatches as the Hendrickson, Olive, Caddis, Cahill, Brown Drake, Pale Evening Dun, Slate Drake,

Caenis, March Brown, White Miller, and various others not yet identified. Hatches begin in March and continue through November. Minute hatches exist all year round. The richness of this environment must be seen to be believed. It would be a pleasure for me to serve as escort to any newcomer to the Breeches who wishes to know something of its potential.

But I've been digressing before I've even gotten to the subject of this chapter. Let's proceed.

Eventually my collection of tried and proved midges had grown to about a dozen. It was a good feeling to know that even if there wasn't a large hatch on the water, I could still expect to take trout on one or another of the new midges. I was having an exceptional run of good fishing. I had almost forgotten what it's like to experience a frustrated, fishless evening. Weeks had passed since that had last happened. I was overconfident.

Late one afternoon JoAnn and I were fishing the Breeches in anticipation of a hatch of white mayflies (*Ephoron leukon*) that would be on the water that evening. The hatch was two hours off, but the fish were visibly feeding on something.

"Try a nymph just below the surface," I called to JoAnn. "They're probably taking the drifting nymphs just under the surface film."

Fifteen minutes later neither of us had had a touch.

"What are they doing?" JoAnn asked.

"Don't ask me," I said. I snipped off a size-14 tan nymph and replaced it with a cream-colored nymph of the same size.

"The white flies will be off tonight, won't they?" she asked.

"Yep," I said, and made a good cast to a rise close to the bank. The nymph was ignored.

Ten more minutes of fishing produced nothing. Enough of this, I thought, reeling in line and watching the water for drifting nymphs.

I was so intent on finding the nymph of the white fly that everything else on the water went unnoticed. I was looking for a size-14 nymph and, one way or another, that's what I was going to see. What fools these mortals be, indeed. Shakespeare wasn't referring to fishermen in particular, but he should have been.

"What do you see?" JoAnn called.

"Nothing."

"They're eating something."

"Now that's good thinking," I mumbled. "Damn right they're eating something. But what?"

I heard a fish splash and turned to register my annoyance with my wife for hooking the first fish. Unnoticed, Rich and Norm Shires had entered the stream below us and had been watching our fishless performance. Rich was playing a good trout.

"What did you get him on?" I hollered.

"Little white midge. Size twenty-eight. They're all over the place."

I could have cheerfully stuck my head under water and not brought it up again.

"They've been on for a couple of nights," Rich commented.

Sure enough, the little white flies were everywhere. It is astonishing how something can escape your notice if you're not looking for it. Rich had spotted them several seasons before and had tied up some excellent imitations. The little whites come and go throughout the season. When they're on the water, they're on in quantity, and the trout gorge themselves. I had a few very small white midges in my fly box. Thanks to Rich and Norm's appearance we managed to take several trout before the big white flies appeared.

Tying the White Midge
Hook—20-28
Thread—white nymph thread
Tail—white hackle fibers
Hackle—white

Insert hook in vise and attach tying thread directly above barb of hook.

Select three hackle fibers and tie on tail.

Wrap an evenly tapered body of white thread forward to the eye of the hook.

Select proper size hackle and strip fibers from the base. Tie in hackle and clip excess stem.

Wrap two turns of hackle, tie off, half hitch, and clip off excess tip.

Wrap head of thread, whip finish, and apply head cement.

the
little olive

If for some mysterious reason I could fish only three fly hatches, I'd unhesitantly choose the little olive as one of them. It would take me a lot longer to decide what the other two would be. How much added pleasure fishermen could enjoy if the olives (the various species of the *Baetis* genus of mayflies) were a prominent hatch all over America. Certain writers have suggested that trout have taste preferences among insects, and casual observation bears this out. Trout seem to have a particular fondness for the little olives.

For years I suspected that wings are unnecessary on dry flies. Part of this attitude stemmed from the fact that I am lazy at the tying bench. Wings take a long time to dress, and I especially begrudge the time when it could be better spent at the stream. And since we all lose a lot of flies, the effort is often wasted. There are some flies that I still tie without wings. I think they take trout just as well without them. But I've changed my views about some others.

In 1966 I gave my theory a test during an olive hatch on the Yellow Breeches. This experience convinced me that wings are needed on certain flies and that they're especially necessary on the olives.

I was fishing a stretch of quiet water on the Breeches one afternoon when the olives started to hatch. Soon *fourteen* trout were rising within thirty yards of where I stood. They had taken up positions close in to the bank, most under some sort of overhanging cover, and were feeding at a rise rhythm of three or four takes a minute.

This sort of heavy hatch often turns accomplished anglers into apparent novices who manage to hook only a few trout despite the boiling activity all around them. More care is required during a heavy hatch than at any other time, so don't blunder about and thrash the water to a froth. Though the trout may *seem* heedless, convince yourself that they're not and act accordingly—be cautious in your approach and make every cast count.

Be calm and logical. Take a good look at the emerging flies and determine their size. Note their wing and body colors. The wings of the olives will always be dun colored, but the bodies may vary from light to dark tan with a definite olive cast. Wings will be from about the length of the body to half again body length. Select the closest imitation you have. Your tippet should be 6X at least, and 7X is even better.

In my experience, trout feeding on olives are ultraselective. I've read that trout become gluttonous and lose all caution during a heavy hatch, but I'm sure that however gluttonous they may get, they remain their usually suspicious selves. The cast and float must be perfect. A dragging fly will be ignored. The fly must ride high on a sparse dressing; olives are delicate little creatures, and an overdressed fly is almost worthless. You can expect success only if your approach, cast, and float are perfect.

So there I was, surrounded with moiling and broiling trout and wading and casting with all the care I could manage. I was fishing a size-18 light-colored wingless dun attached to the leader by a piece of "invisible" sewing thread. (Invisible Sewing Thread is manufactured by the Gudebrod Bros. Company. You can find it at most sewing-notions store counters. It makes an exceptionally flexible tippet material of about 7X diameter, though it's a bit stronger than 7X nylon leader material.) The first trout I approached refused dozens of drag-free floats. He'd come up, look at the fly, and drop back without a touch. I changed to a darker-bodied olive with a mixture of dun and olive hackle, still without wings. Once more, the best I could get from the trout was a cautious inspection. O.K., I thought, let's give this one a rest and try for another. But the next trout was as skeptical as the first. Both went on gulping in every natural that came down their lines of drift. Two other trout were equally disobliging.

It seemed that every trout in the stream was up and feeding. Gulp, sip, gulp, sip. No matter where I looked, flies were disappearing. Glancing through my fly box, I found a size-18 winged olive that Ed Shenk had given me one day on the LeTort. I decided to try it. The next trout I cast to took the fly. Three more followed in about as many casts, each sipping in the imitation as willingly as you please. My prejudice against wings was weakening.

I struck the next trout too fast and snatched the fly out of his mouth. The next was spooked when I dropped my leader in a ball on his head. Success was making me careless.

The next was a good fish, a three-year holdover of about eighteen inches. This was not our first encounter. Three years of looking over flies had made him wise. His lair was a particularly tough one to reach. He was in his usual observation post, tight in to the bank and behind an overhanging branch that almost touched the water. I lit my pipe and watched him feed. Perhaps today I could reach him. All the regulars on the Breeches knew him but none intimately, since no one had been able to invade his domain. There seemed to be two alternatives—either I could try to drop my fly in the dime-sized spot in his window that was open to a cast or I could place the olive at the end of the branch and hope it would lure him from his sanctuary. Neither approach had worked before, and I doubted that they'd work now.

Suddenly I remembered an incident that happened one day while I was fishing with Dick Wood. I had shown Dick a good trout that was finning indolently under a willow sweeper and had let him size up the situation himself. The trout's lie seemed an impossible place to reach with a fly. Dick looked the fish over, remarked that he was a good one, all right, and began to false cast. Dick is a master angler in both fresh and salt water. He handles fly, plug, and spinning gear with equal ease. I've seen him give an object lesson to many an overconfident angler, myself included.

To my surprise, Dick shot the line past the end of the branch and well beyond the trout. The little artificial cricket hit the water a good fifteen feet upstream from the trout's position.

"What are you trying to do?" I yelled. "He's under the limb."

Dick's only reply was an ironical glance. His line began to drag almost immediately. It seemed ridiculous to try to fool a big brown with a dragging fly.

"You'll put him down the minute you pick up that line," I said.

"Watch," he said. Just then he twitched his rod to the left several times, as though trying to make a sidearm roll cast.

The line looped over toward the branch and went slack in the current, and the cricket floated as naturally as could be. But within a few more feet it started to drag again. By this time the line had drifted under the branch. Again Dick gently rolled a few sideways loops into the line, and the cricket slowed to a natural drift within a foot of the trout.

"Come on, you rascal, take it," I said, afraid the cricket would start dragging again. The big jaws opened, the gills flared, and the cricket vanished, leaving a bubble on the surface. Dick struck, and the trout zoomed far in under the limb. Dick and the trout were joined by a 6X tippet, and the trout was wallowing heavily under the trailing branch. I doubted that Dick could extract him. "Well, at least you fooled him," I said.

Dick arched his seven-foot Fenwick for all it was worth and turned the brown into open water. He must have come within an ounce of snapping the tippet. Now Dick could handle him. Ten minutes later the trout gave up. I watched Dick net a burly holdover of nearly four pounds.

"Pretty neat, huh?" was his only comment. He released the trout.

I had learned something worth remembering. Dick's problem then was identical with the one that faced me now, and his ingenious technique might work for me.

My first cast went far to the side, and though I flipped the line over three times, and got a good float each time, the fly drifted wide of the brown's feeding lane. I waited till the fly was far past the trout before making my pickup. The next cast placed the fly well up in front of the branch and just inches from the bank. My line lay close to the end of the branch and angled in toward the bank. Again I rolled the line under the branch. The line went slack, and the olive came right down the chute. "Oh, boy, let it work, let it work," I whispered. The brownie moved sideways and tilted up under the fly. No hesitation, no drifting back, no inspection—he just took. I used the slip strike to set the hook.* Off he went, straining toward the safety of a brush pile well upstream. I put on all the pressure I dared and turned him in time. For several minutes he hung in midstream, trying to inch forward, but the pull of the rod and the press of the current were too much for him. He turned downstream, and after that it was just a matter of time. He measured eighteen and a half inches and weighed almost three and a half pounds.

There were still trout feeding after I got him in, but the little olive was chewed beyond using. It had been a great afternoon. I was content to go home and whip out a few size-18 *winged* olives.

*See p. 151.

Tying the Little Olive

Hook—18 to 22
Thread—olive nymph thread
Tail—blue dun hackle fibers
Body—blend of olive and tan spun fur
Wings—blue dun hackle points
Thorax—blend of olive and tan spun fur
Hackle—blue dun
Head—olive nymph thread

Insert hook in vise and attach thread directly above barb of hook.

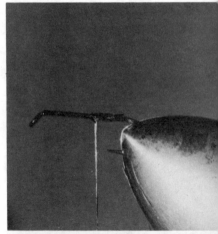

Select a half dozen blue dun hackle fibers for tail and tie in.

Dub small amount of blended fur on thread, wrap body three-quarters of the way toward eye of hook, and half hitch.

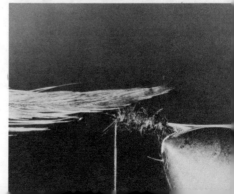

Select two large hackles from dun neck. Measure tips of hackles along shank of hook. Wings should be as long as hook shank.

Tie in hackle tip wings with tips pointed forward over eye of hook.

Clip off excess stem.

Hold wings upright and wrap eight or ten turns of thread in front of stem to make wings stand upright.

When wings are in upright position, split them with dubbing needle. Hold one wing in left hand. Wrap three turns of thread in front of wing in left hand and behind stem of other wing. Next reverse procedure and wrap three turns behind wing that was held in left hand and in front of other wing, forming a crisscross X pattern around the wings.

When wings are in place, dub small amount of fur on thread and wrap in front and back of wings to form thorax.

Tie in hackle behind wings and clip off excess hackle stem. Wrap two turns behind wing and two turns in front. Tie off and clip away excess tip.

Wrap head, whip finish, and apply head cement. Fly is complete.

Caenis
(Tricorythodes)

Where it occurs, this little fly is about equal in importance to the olives in its value to trout and fishermen. The hatches must be seen to be believed. They last only an hour or two, but the number of insects present is immense, and the trout love them.

This miniature mayfly is popularly spoken of as the *Caenis*, but though it's a member of the family of *Caenidae*, it belongs to a different genus, that of the *Tricorythodes*. The true *Caenis* is seen much less frequently than the *Tricorythodes* and doesn't hatch in such huge numbers. But popular usage has mistakenly sanctioned the name *Caenis* for the *Tricorythodes*, and *Caenis* it is likely to remain.

This hatch doesn't occur on all trout waters, so many fishermen aren't familiar with it and don't look for it. However, *Tricorythodes* hatches take place on many streams in the northern United States, among them the Battenkill in Vermont and the Ausable in New York. *Tricorythodes* will usually be found on spring creeks that remain consistently cold. It is present on several central Pennsylvania waters. In the East the hatch may begin in mid-June and carry well into August and September. Some old-timers claim it hangs on till November.

The *Tricorythodes* hatch is unusual, to say the least. The emergence, mating, and spinner fall all take place within a few hours. The trout appear to anticipate the daily coming of the flies, for they will readily take an imitation at the very beginning of a hatch. In fact, more trout can be taken in the early stages of the hatch. When the hatch is at its height the water is so thickly sprinkled with naturals that an imitation is likely to be overlooked. Nevertheless, a properly equipped fisherman can have some of the most fantastic dry-fly fishing imaginable throughout the hatch and spinner fall.

The hatch begins around 8:00 a.m. in June and starts progressively later as the season goes on. By August the hatch starts at around 11:00 a.m. or later. Calm, bright days are best. On windy days the delicate little flies are blown hither and yon, from stream to bank and back again.

There are several species of *Tricorythodes*, and they differ slightly in appearance. For instance, the *Tricorythodes* on Falling Springs is not the same fly that appears on the Yellow Breeches. Generally, though, a good imitation for one stream will work well on another. The specimens I've gathered are about an eighth of an inch long, tails included. The wings are about a quarter of an inch long and appear oversized for the body length. The tails and wings of the duns vary from medium to light gray. Sometimes an off-white hackle will work. The abdomen is white with distinct narrow black ribbing. Occasionally a sparsely dressed size 22 will bring fish, but a 24 is much better, and a Mustad 26 is best if you can find them. As I mentioned in another chapter, 26s are currently available from the Orvis Company.   This hatch is uniquely consistent. *Tricorythodes* appears at a predictable time every day. It's best to be on the stream at the beginning of the hatch. That's when the regular surface feeders take up their stations. As the duns begin to emerge, the sipping rises can be spotted. These early feeders are overeager and very susceptible to imitations. Since few naturals are yet on the water, almost every fly to ride the surface is taken.

As the drifting flies increase in numbers, more and more rising trout appear. At the height of the hatch a twenty-yard stretch where normally only two or three fish are rising will show a dozen or more, all frantically feeding. It's not unusual to see a single trout rising thirty to forty times a minute. Trout are often taken with their stomachs and throats so stuffed with *Tricorythodes* that the insides of their mouths are covered with tiny insects, waiting to be swallowed. One wonders why a trout with that much food in his belly would continue to feed.

By the time the duns are at their greatest numbers, the first flies hatched have completed the mating flight and are falling on the water as spinners. Now the trout have an easier meal. The rise to the spinners is more violent than the rise to the duns. It's often frustratingly difficult to get a take on a spinner when the fall is heaviest. A short stretch of water may be dotted with hundreds of spinners. As the spinner fall heightens, the trout become even more gluttonous. Trout of up to twenty inches can be found in vulnerable feeding stations. Even as the spinner fall tapers off, any trout still rising can be taken with a well-placed cast.

Fishing the *Tricorythodes* hatch is different in general technique from any other sort of fly fishing. Casts should be short—thirty feet at most and often as short as ten. A float of several feet is considered long. Time after time the angler casts, allows a short drift, picks up, and casts again. The more casts made, the more water covered and the better one's chances of fooling a trout. Some of the regulars on our local streams choose a short stretch of water where flies and trout are evident in good numbers, then sit on the grass and fish without moving for two hours, covering only about thirty feet of water. A dozen trout taken and released in one such session is considered a good average morning's fishing.

If you were to ask a dozen different fishermen for advice about the best *Tricorythodes* imitation, you'd probably receive a dozen different answers and be shown as many different patterns. No doubt they all would work more or less well, depending on the fisherman.

My fishing friends and I have found the following pattern to be effective, easy to tie, and durable. Durability is especially important in this pattern. A single hooked fish will leave your fly matted and disheveled. A fly that will still float well after being dried and redressed is quite an asset. A Kleenex or a shirttail will do for touching up a mussed fly. If you have to tie on a new imitation after each trout is released, you'll spend half your fishing time changing flies.

Tying the *Tricorythodes*

TRICORYTHODES DUN
Hook—22 to 26
Thread—black nymph thread
Tail—blue dun hackle fibers
Abdomen—black nymph thread
Thorax—black dubbed fur
Hackle—blue dun

TRICORYTHODES SPINNER
Hook—22 to 26
Thread—white nymph thread
Tail—white hackle fibers
Abdomen—white nymph thread
Thorax—black dubbed fur
Hackle—white

Insert hook in vise and attach tying thread above barb of hook.

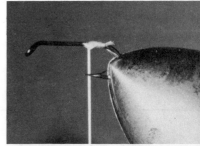

Select several hackle fibers for tail and measure along hook shank. Tail should be slightly longer than hook shank.

Wrap body of thread forward to eye of hook.

Dub small hump of black fur for thorax.

Select proper sized hackle. Strip off soft fibers and tie in hackle butt directly behind thorax.

Wrap two or three turns over thorax, tie off, and clip away excess.

Finish head of thread, whip finish, and apply head cement.

For spinner, clip V in top and bottom of hackle to give spent-wing effect.

notes
on tackle

Much has been written about the sort of tackle best suited for midge fishing. There are a few points of controversy, but experienced fishermen are generally agreed that midges are best fished with the delicate presentation that ultralight tackle makes possible—small flies and light tippets call for light lines and short, light rods. Midges *can* be fished with standard tackle, but the ultimate pleasure comes from refining your line, rod, and reel to match your terminal tackle and fly.

Midge fishing has usually been thought of as difficult. It isn't, really. Nymph fishing, for example, is far more demanding. Any fisherman who gives the midge a fair trial for a season's fishing will find that he has become fairly competent.

Lines

To put your fly down with a minimum of disturbance, a light line must be used. A five-weight line will do nicely, but a four weight is even better. A few fishermen use a three-weight line, though rods capable of casting a three line are not always easy to find. A two-weight line and a rod that will handle it are available, but it seems to me that with such gear one is working a little too close to the limits of the possible. Whether you use a double-taper or a weight-forward line depends on your preference. In my opinion, a double taper has the edge because it's easier to handle when making the short casts that are the rule in midge fishing.

Whatever you do, be sure to match your rod with a line of the proper weight. Many rods have the correct line weight marked on them. If you're having trouble finding the right line weight for your rod, consult a reputable tackle dealer. A rod and line that are mismatched are almost worse than useless. A good procedure is to choose your line weight first and then buy a rod that will handle it.

Rods

Fifteen or twenty years ago, midge-type rods of six to six and a half feet were almost impossible to find. Fishermen who fancied such rods had to either make their own or go to a custom rod maker. Today the picture has changed. Many rod makers now have midge rods available, in either one- or two-piece models.

I was introduced to the midge rod by Ed Shenk, of Carlisle, Pennslyvania. Years ago he made two short, ultralight one-piece glass rods that handled an E-level line. Three- and four-weight lines were unheard of at the time. Occasionally he was able to find an English double-tapered silk line in a size that was perfect for these short rods. He preferred the one-piece sticks to the ferruled models because metal ferrules have a deadening effect on the action of very short rods. Today, of course, glass-on-glass ferrules have changed all that.

Readers who know Ed Shenk will attest to the fact that he is a master of fly casting, especially with the midge rod. He can cast six feet of leader or sixty feet of line with the same faultless ease. He has done more to popularize the short, light rod than anyone I know.

The small rods work best with a medium to slow action. In other words, the flex of the rod should run fairly smoothly from the rod tip to the butt. Rods in which the flex occurs mostly in the upper third of the stick are not well suited to midge fishing. Rods with a tip diameter of 5/64 of an inch and a butt diameter of from .400 to .425 of an inch produce the best action. The handle should be entirely of cork, with two sliding metal bands for the reel seat. A rod of this type will weigh between one and two ounces.

An angler with a reasonable amount of experience using midge equipment will find that ultralight tackle is no harder to use than standard trout gear. Casting techniques for the midge rods are just the same as with standard tackle. The techniques are the same, but the short rod and necessarily short line length require a faster casting cycle. The normal casting range in midge fishing is from twenty to thirty feet. The forty- and fifty-foot casts that one uses with standard tackle are rarely called for. A pickup of twenty-five feet is about the maximum possible. Accuracy and delicacy are far more important than distance.

Reels

All that need be said about reels is that they should be small and single-action. There are a half dozen single-actions on the market today that weigh between two and four ounces.

Leaders

There has been a good deal of controversy over the correct design of a good fly leader. First off, there are two types of tapered leaders—knotless and knotted. I recommend knotted leaders. Knotless tapers are less expensive, but that's their only advantage, so far as I'm concerned. Knotted leaders can be either bought custom tied or made up at home. A good custom-tied composite leader will cost from 75¢ to $1.50. If you buy leader material in bulk and tie your own composites, they'll be considerably cheaper. I've found that knotted leaders will turn over and lay out a fly more consistently and more exactly than the knotless type. Also, if the tippet is snapped off a knotted leader, replacement is quite simple, since the angler knows (or should know) the diameter of the leader at the point where it broke. Without a micrometer to give an exact reading, the angler who repairs a knotless leader will very likely ruin the taper. A custom-tied or home-tied knotted leader should last an entire season if the last three sections are periodically replaced. And knotted leaders float better than the knotless kind.

In general, and up to a certain point, the longer the leader the better. Most commercial leaders come in seven-and-a-half, nine, and twelve-foot lengths. I suggest nine feet as the minimum length for midges, and fifteen feet is sometimes not too long. You're usually safe with a twelve-foot leader. Tippet sizes of either 5X or 6X are best to start with. If conditions make it necessary for you to fish finer, you can cut back your tippet and add lighter material, using the familiar blood knot and working down to 7X or 8X. The butt section of the leader (the end that attaches to the fly line) should be about .002 to .004 of an inch smaller than the line point. This usually indicates a leader butt of either .019 or .021. The following leader formulas are the most effective I've come across. If you find that you have to refine your leader, just cut back the tippet to six inches and add twenty-four inches to the next smaller size.

10 feet, 6X
(1) 48"−.019
(2) 18"−.015
(3) 12"−.013
(4)   6"−.011
(5)   6"−.009
(6)   6"−.007
(7) 24"−.005

12 feet, 7X
(1) 54"−.021
(2) 24"−.017
(3) 12"−.013
(4) 10"−.011
(5)   8"−.009
(6)   6"−.007
(7)   6"−.005
(8) 24"−.0037

Many fishermen find that when they first begin using fine tippets they often break fish off on the strike. They find it difficult to strike promptly without striking so hard as to pop the tippet. The answer to this dilemma is the slip strike. Here's how you do it. As you strip in line, keep the line between the cork rod grip and the second finger of your rod hand. When a trout takes, raise your rod tip smartly while simultaneously releasing the second finger's hold on the line. Raising the rod will start the line moving toward you. Releasing the line will allow the line to slide up through the guides. The line will be drawn toward you faster than it goes out the guides, so that when contact is made with the fish, the hook will be set firmly but without the sudden shock that often snaps the leader. Once mastered, this technique will result in more hooked trout and fewer broken tippets than you ever imagined possible.

Falling Spring, Pennsylvania, one of the finest and most productive streams in the East.

*Ed Koch is here shown casting on a favorite stretch
of Falling Spring.*

A trout can often be unhooked in the net and released without ever being touched by hand.

*A properly released trout almost always survives,
often to be caught and released again.*